BEDFORDSHIRE
FOLK
TALES

BEDFORDSHIRE FOLK TALES

JEN FOLEY

ILLUSTRATED BY TONY HUNT

For my Uncle John,
one of the best and funniest storytellers
I've ever known, and loving to the last.

First published 2015

The History Press
The Mill, Brimscombe Port
Stroud, Gloucestershire, GL5 2QG
www.thehistorypress.co.uk

© Jen Foley, 2015

The right of Jen Foley to be identified as the Author
of this work has been asserted in accordance with the
Copyright, Designs and Patents Act 1988.

British Library Cataloguing in Publication Data.
A catalogue record for this book is available from the British Library.

ISBN 978 0 7509 6223 0

Typesetting and origination by The History Press
Printed in Great Britain

CONTENTS

ACKNOWLEDGEMENTS

Thank you to Liz Pieksma, Keeper of Archaeology and Lydia Saul, Keeper of Social History at The Higgins, Bedford, and to the staff at the Bedfordshire Archive for their patience and attention to detail. Also to Aragon Lace Makers for their skill and hospitality.

Thank you to Tony Hunt, my illustrator, for his skill, expertise and patience. His illustrations have brought the stories to life.

Finally I am grateful to Fibs and Fables storytelling group, who introduced me to the wonderful world of oral storytelling and to everyone who read my stories and kept me going whilst I put the stories down on paper.

Introduction

These stories are those of ordinary people in extraordinary circumstances throughout the centuries. These are not just the stories of lords and ladies, but of invaders, travellers, yeomen, highwaymen and saints.

The county of Bedfordshire has been described as unassuming and modest but that is deceptive. The chalk downs, the clay vales, and the ridges provide a rich setting for Bedfordshire's folklore past. Many of its treasures are found at the end of an obscure path or by opening a gate to enter seemingly unassuming church grounds.

Tales have been told to explain ghostly presences, the scenery, and the history of Bedfordshire. Whether it be snippets of talk in town or round-the-fire sessions at the farm, the people of Bedfordshire have always enjoyed a good yarn, embellishing and entertaining. The emerging folk tales reflect the ingenuity and the creativity of its people.

Jen Foley, 2015

1

THE FLAMING GIBBET OF GALLEY HILL

John rubbed his forehead anxiously, taking off his glasses and staring at the figures dancing in front of his dazed eyes. The door behind him was closed and beyond that he could hear the sound of his children's muffled giggling as they slid down the banisters. He smiled to himself, thinking about the onrush of children since his marriage, which was why he was here, looking at figures written on crisp white paper. They were not giving a pretty picture. Maybe he should think about the proposition that had been made to him, but that was risky and illegal. With a sigh, he shut the book and closed the study door behind him, going to join the rest of his family. There was a squeal of delight from Jack and Maisie as he pretended to be shocked and chased them down the stairs.

John was a Luton merchant. When he had fallen in love, he had fallen quick and fast, and promised himself that he would let his wife have whatever she wanted. Adjusting his cuffs, he strode towards his warehouse, but he couldn't stop mulling over the effect that the other merchants' wives were having on his debts. His wife expected him to buy whatever they had and he had done nothing to stop that expectation. While she was happy, deliriously so, he knew that they faced bankruptcy and that all their fine things – their private possessions, their beds and their clothes – would then be sold publicly in the market place. Their lives on show.

When he reached his warehouse he pulled open the gates to the tang of street smells masked by the fresh scent of straw. He barely registered the smells, however, he was so deeply lost in thought. Talking with his foreman later in the morning, an idea started to crystallise. He was used to organising the arrival and despatch of goods but, because of taxes, the profit was thin. Why not put his experience to good use? The problem with that had always been storage. His wife might not be worldly but even she would start to ask questions if their cellar was full of barrels of whiskey and boxes of tea. A constant chameleon, she described herself as a realist, a pragmatist, hard-headed or sensitive, it really depended on the company she was with at the time. Yet he nevertheless felt a tug of protectiveness. He would shield her from the threat of bankruptcy. With a bit of subterfuge and smart-talking, he had found the perfect way of keeping smuggled goods. It was so deliciously ironic; he would fool Luton's townspeople with their own superstition. He hadn't been to church for years but he thought of praying now and thanking God. But then he didn't know what was to come.

In September, the talk began. For years there had been stories of a duke who had failed to support his ally in the Cousins' War and paid for it with his life in the grounds of Someries Castle. Now there were signs that his ghost had been reawakened. There were rumours aplenty of sightings of dragons, dead animals found in the grounds of the castle and strange noises in the middle of the night. Soon local people started to avoid the area, especially at night.

It was one of John's great joys in life to ask locals about the strange drumming heard from Someries, knowing that his men would simultaneously be moving barrels of whiskey from wagons and drumming in the ruins to keep away locals. The castle was abandoned a couple of decades ago and partially demolished. The crumbling pockmarked walls offered little protection against

the elements but some rooms remained complete. Together with
the warren of underground tunnels and basements, John had plenty
of space to store the whiskey, tea and silk that the townspeople
of Luton craved. There were even arrow-slits, originally built for
dramatic effect, which his men used to survey the surroundings.

Over the next couple of months, magistrates started to notice
that tea and silk had become much more available in the town.
In one part of town, a rather bulky woman knocked politely
on the door of the local drapers. With the minimum of noise,
the draper's wife let her in. Both women proceeded upstairs to a
storeroom where the bulky woman took off her outer dress and
then lifted up her arms. This was the signal for the shopkeeper
to grasp the end of the length of material that had been coiled
around the other woman. As she spun, the shopkeeper released
the silk and scooped it up into the air. Like butterflies suddenly
taking flight, the air was now ablaze with colour and movement,
and both women were quite giddy with the sight of all this luxury
floating around them. In another part of town, a lady in wide
skirts visited the grocer. She was ushered into one of the back
rooms and quickly took off her skirt, revealing petticoats with
pockets sewn into them. Quickly the pair moved the tea from
the pockets into one of the wooden drawers. As the lady left the
grocer's wife rubbed her hands together with glee. The ladies in
elegant drawing rooms, sipping tea from fragile bone-china cups,
would pay a pretty price for this tea.

Thus began the halcyon days, when the living was easy. No one was hurt, the shopkeepers had whiskey, tea, silk and tobacco at a reasonable price and everyone in the smuggling chain benefited. John's family got whatever they hinted they wanted and his wife never needed to worry about keeping up with her set of friends. The method of distribution seemed unassailable because of its inventiveness. The customs men were just as superstitious as the townspeople and so would never explore the castle, and they were looking for barrels and boxes in the distribution rather than women. Everything was going well until a new man joined them.

The slight man seemed harmless at first. He looked as if he would collapse at the slightest weight, and indeed he was never given the job of carrying a barrel on his back, but he was quick. His feet were quick and his mind was quick as well. John would reel off instructions with barely a pause and the man would be able to repeat them back to another word for word. John found himself able to enjoy life more, as the new man gradually oiled the wheels of the operation. He had more time to unwind with his family because of the man's sheer efficiency. The man gained the nickname 'Numbers' because of his ease with figures. Soon he was at the heart of the operation, so John was surprised when he received an anonymous note saying that Numbers was a customs man.

John toyed with the idea of taking Numbers to France and abandoning him. But with Numbers' fierce intelligence he knew that he would understand the lie of the land quickly. He would only find a way to earn a living and come back to England to denounce him. For weeks he thought of other ways to get rid of Numbers and, at the same time, he feared Numbers would uncover the whole operation. The price and penalty for smuggling was death, the same as murder. Inevitably his mind was drawn down the logical path that if by smuggling he was considered akin to a murderer, then he might as well be a murderer. Once he had had that thought then it could not be undone. He bought his wife a new dinner set, hid it with a tablecloth and revealed the gift with a flourish. As she thanked him with a kiss that promised something more, he thought that ridding himself of Numbers would give her and his family security. Overlooking a delivery of whiskey, he thought that this could all soon be lost unless he did indeed rid himself of Numbers.

Soon Numbers became his right-hand man and John spread the word that he would be going into semi-retirement, leaving Numbers as the de facto head. Numbers now knew that either the game was up and he needed to gather as much information as he could and leave discreetly or John had indeed given him the chance to infiltrate the whole smuggling network. This could be the chance to make his mark within the service, the story that would be his calling card and his fortune. It could be the end of his career or even his life.

John, in his semi-retirement, gave Numbers a set of books for customs and another set of books with cryptic references. Numbers gradually deciphered the references to show the runs from the coast, who they came from and the goods expected. He let it be known to the coastal men that by adding some extra ingredients, he could increase the profits for all. The stage was set for a sacking.

Late one night both men were summoned to the castle by men higher up the smuggling chain. John looked around in the half-light. He saw the shadowy figures ahead of him, with Numbers standing next to the coastal men chatting easily. The figure that was clearly the leader started to ask John questions, he found that his palms were sweating, his voice was higher as he started to justify himself and how he had set up the operation. Now he feared that Numbers was not a customs man but a competitor or a customs man who had been tempted. Then he heard a crack as a hand reached back and pistol-whipped Numbers around the head. They rolled him over and, with a man hooking an arm under each shoulder, he was dragged away. Numbers stared at John, more shocked than reproachful, and after a short silence, laughter resounded. John heard the sound of the man screaming as he was tortured for information but the sound was dulled by the beating of his heart. He waited until it had gone quiet, staggered home, and drank himself into a stupor, falling asleep on the floor.

When he woke up the next morning, as soon as he opened his eyes the memories of the day before began whispering, clamouring and murmuring in his head. He took a hip flask with him into the depot and when these memories started to surface, he took a quick nip from the flask. When a runner came up to him asking for Numbers, the fear he felt was overpowering. He struggled to answer calmly. For the first time in his life he needed a drink to keep his agitation under control. A small voice in his head told him that this would be brought to an end with arrest as a smuggler.

Each following day, he needed just a little more drink to stop the clamouring voices getting ever louder inside his head. His wife started to notice when he forgot to buy a birthday present for their son. She shrugged it off and made excuses to the boy, placating him with assurances of treats to come. Increasingly she found his behaviour erratic – either needy and wanting her company, or sulky and rejecting her. The problem for John was that the world was full of reminders. Passing a message to the man who replaced Numbers was a reminder, someone of the same build was a reminder, the fact that he still had his beautiful house was a reminder.

When he found himself stumbling out of a squalid gamblers den, drunk and barely able to find his way home, he knew he needed to make a drastic change and save his family. Eventually he set up a meeting with the coastal smugglers and explained that he wanted to get out, he would do whatever they wanted to move away and be free of his past. He had expected anger but the man laughed in his face and that was when he was told that Numbers had not died quickly. John had left the depot when Numbers had lost consciousness. Later they had tortured him further and he had revealed names, addresses and places where the men were to be found. John did not have the death of one man on his conscience but eleven.

When John woke up the next morning, the murmuring and clam-ouring voices had become a din that he could no longer control. John could not rid himself of thoughts about the eleven men who had died and he feared that somehow the family of one of those men would learn about him. In a back street, he bought the most vicious-looking dog that he could find for his protection. His wife looked browbeaten when he showed her the animal. He couldn't bear the thought that she felt so intimidated but it was the only way he could walk down the street without showing his fear. When he bought the dog into the bedroom, she took her final exit from the marital bed, saying their son was poorly. The dog now slept by the foot of his bed.

In the days that followed, his control of the whole operation became tenuous. He saw ghosts and customs men behind every corner. Everywhere he went, John took the black dog with him because he constantly feared reprisals. The dog looked fierce but was also incredibly loyal to him and offered him constant and unquestioning companionship.

He did not contain his fear and aggressiveness at the depot. A small boy was cheeky to him and he lost control, shouting in the boy's face and then pushing him to the ground. The boy cowered on the ground and John rushed at him, kicking and screaming until he was pulled away by two men who looked at him with revulsion. The men left the depot, never to be seen again. With the death of eleven men to bear, he thought little of ordering an eviction or the roughing up of a tavern landlord. Where he had been respected, he was now hated.

It was inevitable that he would make enough mistakes to be reported to customs. Before long he was found guilty and taken to the gallows (which stood next to the main road that is now the A6 and called Galley Hill, between the north of the town and Streatley), and here he was hanged.

As an executed criminal, his body was soaked in tar for three days before being bound in chains and hoisted on to the gibbet. That night, black storms clouds gathered and there was a tumultuous storm, wreaking havoc on crops and smashing farm machinery. Suddenly, a bolt of lightning hit the gibbet and the shape of a huge black dog emerged, prancing around in the flames for hours until the fire died down. The terrifying apparition then howled piercingly, leapt on to the ashes and vanished.

Some say that the black dog still found some good within John's soul and prowled for hours to guard against the Devil's approach. Others say that the man was lost and that the dog stayed near him to introduce him to the Devil on his approach. But from then onwards, travellers would find themselves confronted by the most enormous black hound at this spot, which was said to have glowing red eyes and a sinister growl.

2

THE THREE
HIGHWAYMEN

The young woman waiting at the bar of the Flying Horse in Clophill did not take much notice of the three men who arrived at the inn late one night. It had been quiet for most of the evening and she sighed as she smoothed down her apron and tucked her hair back into its ribbon. Such gestures made it clear that, although she was not the tavern owner's wife, she was still respectable. This was not the kind of tavern in which customers could make enquiries of the tavern-owner and expect her company for the night. Sarah was well known in the village for her wit and her ability to say a cheeky remark and then duck as the clip round the earhole from the tavern-owner missed her by a feather's breadth. However, she had been working for hours now and her good

humour had evaporated. She slipped her feet out of her simple shoes and ran her toes along her calf muscles to try and bring them back to life. She was looking forward to the walk back to her mother and father's cottage, crowded though it was.

The new moon, on the cusp of its journey back to fullness, was a flicker of light in the darkness. The men arrived well-mounted, just as the day was turning into bible-black night. The youngest, quietest man, who introduced himself as Jack, followed the stable-lad out into the yard. 'Be sure to put some oats in their feed,' he said, and was answered with a nod and an invitation to check the feed. Jack held the grains in his hands; the kernels were plump and heavy, and gave off a reassuringly clean smell. 'They are warm after riding all day. If they cool down too quickly they may catch a chill,' he added, which provoked a quick spark of irritation stifled by a laugh.

'Don't you worry yourself sir, we look after many horses here and know many have had a long journey.'

At that Jack unwound, and with a friendly pat on the shoulder of the stable-lad, returned to his fellow travellers, who were in fact his brothers.

The three shabbily dressed men told Sarah that they were dealers in horses when she poured ale for them, the bitter-sweet hoppy smell bringing smiles to their faces. As she brought out bread and meat for them, she overheard a bit of their conversation, '… poor sister living with that bastard, will she ever forgive us for making her live with that evil man?' The tallest, brashest brother ordered malt whiskey and she thought of him as 'Boss'. Boss and his ginger-haired stocky brother, who she simply named 'Ginger', brayed about the outrageous behaviour of highwaymen.

'We're afraid to go from fair to fair for fear of them,' they said. 'Hanging is too good for them.'

Jack, meanwhile, cast furtive looks around the tavern and appeared relieved when they ordered in hot punch and headed to bed. The reckoning for themselves and horses was about twelve shillings.

About six o'clock the next morning, they set out with the noise of the horses' hooves clattering on the road and the sound of occasional neighing. It didn't take them long to travel the three miles to Ampthill. They wandered around the fair, nonchalantly and without purpose. They made great show of being buyers, and spent a good amount of time examining horses' hooves and scrutinising their teeth. They stayed some few hours there without buying anything, and then, at about eleven o'clock, they wandered into a butcher's tavern at Houghton Conquest and had cold roast beef for breakfast. When they asked what they could have for dinner, the landlady told them that there was a sheep hanging up in the shop. However, she said, grimacing, her husband was at the fair and she could not cut it. The tallest man of the trio, Boss, then slipped the knife from the butcher's board and, with great skill, he took off the shoulder.

By five o'clock they were waiting on the road. Their dissolute air had now dissipated as they took up positions on the thoroughfare between Ampthill and Bedford in the parish of Houghton Conquest, waiting for travellers to pass. An unwary traveller ambled slowly towards them. The moment swelled and built in anticipation, and they could feel the blood pounding in their ears. The two younger brothers stood blocking the road and Boss held a blunderbuss in open view about twenty yards away from them, his coat billowing in the wind. All was quiet except for bursts of birdsong.

In the distance they saw the small figure getting closer. As he drew nearer to them, they could see that he was well dressed. The man, a tenant of Lord Ashburnham, slowed to a halt with a look of consternation as he realised what lay ahead of him. He gulped and his Adam's apple bobbed up and down as he asked the men how he could help them. With that the tension of the trio dissolved. The younger two emptied the man's pockets as Boss held the blunderbuss aimed at his head. Then Boss offered to give him a pound back from the seventeen that they had stolen from him. The brothers lightly tossed the coin between each other and like 'piggy in the middle' the man hurtled from one to another, trying to intercept the coin as they jeered at him. After they had let him go, they robbed three other people as they came along the road: a dealer in hogs, who lived at Elstow, was relieved of about fifteen pounds; a man from Cardington of about five pounds; and a tradesman from Bedford of about fourteen shillings and his watch. They returned the small coins to their owners, having, as they described it, a little jest each time. Eventually it grew dark, with cloud scuttling across the sky. The highwaymen travelled along the road until they spied the light from a small settlement; there they robbed two farmers of about thirty pounds and a joiner of a few shillings and his watch.

At about nine o'clock they called at an alehouse in Maulden and each drank a glass of gin. From there they continued to the George pub at Silsoe, where they sat on horseback at the door and drank three pints of wine and ate a crust of bread. No words of anger were heard between them, but Jack seemed quiet, sullen and resentful whilst his brothers were full of bonhomie. There was also no sign of any weapons.

The highwaymen's victims, meanwhile, walked to Bedford to raise the hue and cry. The unfortunate men appeared before Mr Edwards, the local magistrate, before leading a search for the men, but by the time the alarm reached Silsoe the next morning, much had changed.

The brother had finished their drinks and intended to ride away from Bedfordshire completely. As the two eldest brothers became more ecstatic, however, the mood of Jack became blacker and sourer. After travelling just a quarter of a mile from the George, he started to mumble angrily to himself until finally, with a vicious look at his eldest brother, he sneered that the eldest was still unable to look after their sister. His brother swerved his horse, pulling the reins high and clenching his fists. Riding with their horses next to one another, the eldest and the youngest brothers edged closer, their faces inches apart and rigid with tension. Staring into his brother's eyes, the eldest challenged the younger, crying, 'Say that again!'

The words burst from Jack's lips explosively, 'The two of you, you told her she was a burden, just another mouth to feed.' He seemed to find his confidence as he said slowly, 'She would never have left without you pushing her. If she dies at his hands, it'll be your fault.'

Boss laughed and his eyes had a coruscating twinkle. He was enjoying himself. That was when little Jack lost control. Later the young man would tell his sister that he had no memory of the scene. How he had punched his brother on the nose so hard that he could feel bone and cartilage crumble like a biscuit. The eldest brother lurched to the ground and Jack pulled out the blunderbuss that his brothers had given him to look after. Truth be told, his brothers only expected him to look after the horses and not to do the man's work of threatening innocent people. Nevertheless, he knew how to use the gun. He took aim and he could feel the rage coursing through his body. He pulled the trigger and shot his eldest brother in the back. His brother, who had begun to push himself up on all fours, slumped on the ground. Jack jumped off his horse and kicked the body over with one foot. It was lifeless and the eyes seemed to be looking into the distance. Within a short time the blood from the body had stained the ground and, along with a shocked and fearful

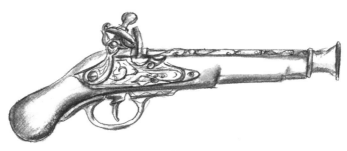

Ginger, Jack dragged the body through a gate into a close just by the roadside, and for reasons he never fully understood, shot him again with a pistol through the head. Local residents at the George pub heard the blunderbuss. Dazed, the brothers rode into the distance, not talking to one another.

A farmer at Barton rode by in the time between the firing of the blunderbuss and the pistol. Unable to see the body and the men in the close, he still smelt the powder and with difficulty got his horse past. Later he said that he thought somebody was shooting wood pigeons. The tollgate man said the farmer had not passed two minutes before the highwaymen came hurtling towards him with a spare horse tied on to the lead horse. They seemed much in haste, but stayed to take their change. They left the saddle upon the downs and the horse at Luton. In the next few hours the horse was claimed and the owner said that the man who had stolen his horse had formerly been a servant of his and was able to give a description of the three brothers.

There were reports of Ginger and the Jack travelling together in the next week and then these dwindled out. Convinced that one or both of the brothers had murdered their elder sibling, a reward was set for both men. Illogically, Jack thought that, as he had spent so much of his life barely noticed, he would miss the attention of any bounty hunters. In no time at all he was captured and the news spread swiftly across Bedfordshire. Ginger was in hiding when he heard of Jack's detainment. He knew that he would be adrift after Jack's death; that he would have nobody left in the world. Boss was already under the ground and his sister Lizzie had told him that he was dead to her. He started to wonder why he should continue. It was at this point that he made the decision that would shape his final days.

Months later, Ginger stood beside the hangman at the gallows. The rope dangled next to him. He turned and, with a remorseful air, begged the hangman to wait a while.

'I am waiting to see my brother and sister,' he said. He had offered himself in place of Jack. By saving his brother, he had given both Jack and his sister Lizzie something to live for. By dying he would give both of them a place of belonging, a family.

Two figures walked slowly towards him. The crowds parted as they explained that they were related to Ginger and several people gave them interested looks. Now they were close enough to look him in the eye.

'Have they come to save you?' asked the hangman. 'No they have not come to bring you silver or any gold. They have come to see me swinging from the gallows.' And at that, the hangman decided he could wait no longer and moved the horse and cart on, leaving the man swinging from the noose.

The rope tightened and pulled on his neck immediately but it was not a merciful death as it failed to break his windpipe. In his dying moments Ginger watched his brother and sister for any sign. His brother looked at him meaningfully and then knelt down to pray. Jack had always felt sympathy for all, the high and low, the powerful and the powerless, man and woman. But when he stared at his sister, Ginger could sense nothing. The terrible pain started to fade as gossamer-like threads dulled his vision and he began to feel a lightness, as if he was about to drift way. He strained for one look of forgiveness from his sister. She had always worn her hair over her face out of shyness but now he feared it was to hide the bruises. As she softly pushed her hair behind her ear, he could see the gentle curve of her mouth and, as the blackness started to fall, he thought he saw a shadow of a wry smile. His sister, it seemed, had damned him to hell while his brother Jack sought divine forgiveness.

3

THE MAI DUN

Bedfordshire is generally a fruitful county, prosperous and fertile. Yet there was a time when it was a bleak place to live. The Roman garrisons – who had just begun to think of the Britons as their neighbours, even if they were not countrymen – had been recalled to Rome. The Britons – who had been lulled into a sense of invulnerability by the Roman Empire – now found themselves defenceless as tribes throughout Europe looked at their lush and green land with interest.

And from this chaos arose one warlord who had the ambition to become King of the Britons. In his inexorable rise, he broke promises, spoke gentle yet empty words of peace, and placed the rise of his family above all else. In the battle for the soul of Britain, Vortigern was formidable.

Vortigern travelled through Bedfordshire, having sent messengers ahead to tell the queen of a local tribe of his arrival. Her husband had died in the previous year, and she had kept to the old ways in claiming his land as hers. Vortigern expected a woman who would jump at the sight of a sheep.

He was surprised, therefore, by the woman that he encountered upon his arrival. Her skin was dark and lined, her hair long, and the fluid way she moved spoke of a person who knew how to draw attention and how to use it to her own advantage. Instead of a mute coward, she was tall, self-possessed, her dark hair falling down in waves. Cynically, Vortigern wondered how much time she had spent mourning her husband. The Druids and warriors looked to her for guidance when he pointedly spoke to them instead of her and they seemed willing to accept her leadership.

Vortigern decided that it was time to be blunt. 'I expect you to submit all of your lands,' he said calmly.

The queen glanced down at the ground. She was unwilling to become a vassal of this man, owing him servitude. It would mean watching the humiliation of her people from the sidelines. The alternative was to fight but that would result in a loss of life that she wanted to avoid.

As she contemplated the ground she murmured, almost to herself, 'Enter a gilded cage or fight, is that it?'

'You will not find a better ruler to provide a gilded cage. What would be so wrong with becoming my vassal queen?' Vortigern immediately countered, and their eyes locked in a battle of wills.

Eventually Vortigern had to look away.

'I'll wager you,' said the queen in the silence that followed, 'I can camp an army within a bull's hide.'

'Do that,' said the surprised Vortigern, 'and I will allow you to retain those men to keep you safe and keep the land as well.' A bull's hide was brought to him and he made an oath in front of his men. Pouring a libation of wine, he swore to keep to this oath in honour of the goddess of his hearth. He left, looking forward to their next meeting.

As soon as he was out of sight, the queen summoned the maidens of her tribe. They scrutinised the cut of the bull's hide before taking the sharpest tools that they had. Then they cut the hide into long and narrow strips. These strips were so thin that they were almost as fine as thread. Then the queen rubbed the strips in red ochre and dexterously joined them together. She ordered the maidens to form a circle on the grass with the cowhide and, rubbing the red ochre on the grass, they created an imprint that followed the exact lines of the hill fort of their ancestors. She summoned labourers and explained that they must create a fortification. It was imperative, she told them, that they should not move outside of the imprint left for them. To do so would risk everything.

For days the men worked, creating a fort that would give their queen a powerbase. Their work did not go unnoticed, however. Vortigern was a dangerous man to cross and the news that the queen had been audacious enough to create such a fort reached him quickly. The queen set up a watch system so that when he arrived, she would be ready to greet him, whether that be day or night.

A short time afterwards, the queen was rudely awoken from her sleep by one of her people shaking her roughly. She rose and prepared herself to meet Vortigern and his men, who were already striding towards the fort. Vortigern confronted her, barely able to contain his rage. 'I gave you the opportunity to surrender and now you have violated our agreement. You and your people will be enslaved and treated without mercy.'

The queen tilted her head to study him. 'On the contrary, I have kept to our agreement. The camp you see before you fits within a bull's hide. We may have strengthened old fortifications but I haven't transgressed.'

Vortigern had never been spoken back to in this way. His eyes narrowed as he looked at her. 'This is going to be entertaining and then I'm going to have you taken away in chains. Explain.'

The queen called one of her maids forward, hiding her misgivings as she did so. 'King Vortigern, I show you the bull hide you left me,' and with a flourish she pulled out the bull hide, which had been taken apart and now resembled a long piece of thread. You will see the shape of our new encampment. We have been very conscientious and I assure you that the space taken is no more than that we can fit within the space created by this bull hide.'

Vortigern's eyes seemed to be burning with rage and the queen and her maids jumped back startled as he threw back his head and laughed. He laughed until he felt weak and sat on the floor to recover his breath. The queen quickly motioned for a servant to bring a beaker of water and knelt in front of him, smiling. It seemed quite spontaneous and ordinary to speak to him as a friend and he looked at her with admiration. In recognition of the queen's skill, he ordered that she be allowed to keep her land and, for the time that Vortigern had left in power, he ensured that she and her tribe were safe.

Today Maiden Bower is described as one of the most significant Iron Age sites in Bedfordshire. There is speculation that the name comes from the Celtic *mai dun*, meaning fortress on the plain, and the word *bower*, meaning a woman's private chamber in a castle.

4

Brotherhood

Caedmon nudged his friend Ælfric, who had been watching a bird
of prey above them. Lying on the forest floor and peering through
the bracken, they had been ordered to watch the Viking fortress
at Tempsford. They had come up the river from Beda's Ford, both
excited about what they might find. The reality of watching the
fortress was different. Waiting for the first signs of activity, they
were now fractious and finding it difficult to cope with the tedium.

When the Vikings had first made a fortress at Tempsford,
Caedmon had felt a pang of fear. Their settlement was next to the
ford and named after the chief Beda, who built it many generations
ago. They were close to the Danelaw land and the Danish Vikings
constantly raided over the border. First the Vikings had built a fortress
at Huntingdon and then abandoned it as they moved to Tempsford
and built the fortress that the young men were looking at now.

As Caedmon fidgeted, trying to get comfortable, he thought of
the stories that had reached the people of Beda's Ford. The farmers
near the fortress had been unwilling to give the Vikings all of their
food and allow their own families to starve. They had launched
an attack despite the Vikings' fighting prowess. The fighting had
been vicious and the poor farmers had suffered. In the winter
since, the Vikings had been a great burden upon the people in the
surrounding countryside as well. They were becoming ever more
audacious with their raids as they came to know the lie of the land.

Caedmon glanced at Ælfric, who was frowning. He recognised that look and hoped that his friend wasn't contemplating some new dangerous scrape. Caedmon tried to stay focused and his eyes roved over the fortress as he sought to overcome his boredom. His lord wanted to destroy it. The fortress was not impregnable, but attackers needed to use the element of surprise and destroying it would be difficult. He turned just in time to see Ælfric shin up a tree. His friend was up to his old tricks again.

Caedmon stayed as still as he could, hoping that nobody noticed Ælfric's foolhardy move. He knew that his friend hoped to get a better idea of the layout of the fortress this way. The young men had trained together as teenagers and learned many life lessons together. He winced as he remembered how they had boasted that together they would be able to take down a whole host of Vikings.

He froze as he noticed two men talking by the ramparts and pointing in their direction. It may be nothing to do with Ælfric's recklessness but the anxiety was now like a barb in his gut. As minutes passed he imagined that the two Vikings were discussing their sighting. If a party of men charged out from the fortress, Ælfric and Caedmon would be hunted down and killed. Caedmon was contemplating shaking the tree or even whispering up to Ælfric when his friend's face appeared through the foliage grinning widely and he clamboured down without incident.

At the end of the day, the pair returned to Beda's Ford. Ælfric was buoyed up by the adventure, exuberant and ready to tell anyone about what he had seen of the fortress. The lord was particularly interested. He granted Ælfric an audience and listened carefully. Ælfric's prominence was short-lived, however, as more and more rumours and stories of the Vikings' outrages poured into Beda's Ford. An attack on their settlement seemed likely, the Vikings had bragged of such a thing. The lord had vowed his revenge on the Danes, promising that he would drag them to their deaths, but first they must defend themselves against the coming attack.

As they cleaned their weapons, Caedmon and Ælfric reminisced about their first battles. How reckless they had been, eager to be the first to run at the enemy, which of course just betrayed a youthful attack of nerves rather than confidence. They had learnt over the years to be good company for each other. Honest yet not burdening the other by dwelling on their fears or thinly covering them with cheerfulness. They played a game of Taefl, almost upending the board in a mock argument and horseplay. Then it was time to prepare their bedding for the night and a young slave brought in food for the group. Caedmon was left with his fears once more and he wondered what he would awake to. He dreaded a visit from the men from the North, who used magic, cavorting with unclean spirits. The fear was so strong that it almost took his mind off the growling, crunching and slobbering noises of his friends eating. Almost, but not quite completely. Noisily, they ate the meat off the animal bones and tossed the bones into the rushes.

Feeling restless, he walked out into the cold, strolling past the huts of many sizes. He almost choked on the invasive smell of the pit that the community used to relieve themselves. It was hidden from sight by a wattle screen but the stench made its use obvious. He looked out over the landscape, flat with the gentle sound of the river flowing nearby.

He returned to the hall. The fire lay smouldering and the group were settling down to sleep. Carefully he lay down his drinking cup and plate. The drinking cup was finely decorated. At first he had been proud that he could afford such a possession, but now he took it for granted. As he prepared his bedding, he was more aware of the slight light-headedness he felt from the beor. Although tired, sleep did not come easily, he could hear the sound of his fellow warriors snoring, seemingly unperturbed by the coming danger. As he became drowsy, he thought he heard the sound of wolves in the distance.

He was jolted awake by the unholy din of metal thundering on metal. Overwhelmed by the noise, he looked around to see other warriors also stumbling out of their bedding, clutching their weapons. Some briefly kissed amulets before tucking them out of sight into clothing. The alarm had been sounded. What would they face as they rushed out into the night? Maybe one or two Vikings, maybe they could meet a small army.

A young lad was waiting for them by the doors of the great hall. He was a churl, the lowest level of freedman, but ambitious to prove himself with his lord. Deferentially, and remarkably quickly, he explained the system of birdcalls that they had used to warn of the approach of the Vikings. He pointed east towards a patch of open land.

They were skirting around the side of the woodland, hoping to keep some natural cover, when Caedmon looked across the clearing. His eyes had adjusted to the semi-darkness now and he could sense small changes in the light as patterns coalescing around the trees. He watched transfixed as those patterns gathered around the emerging figures of the Vikings. From different ends of the clearing, both sides moved into battle formation, but still kept their distance. They could see some of the younger Viking warriors searching for stones and rocks. His mouth felt dry as he watched them approach.

They stood steadfast as stones and axes hailed upon them. He was tempted to run but it was a ridiculous and fleeting thought – it would mean humiliation for himself and his family. The more seasoned warriors did not flinch; their minds seemed to be elsewhere. Caedmon started to mutter a prayer to one of the old goddesses. Although his chief called such prayers magic and said they should be praying to the Christian God, he knew that many of his fellow warriors kept amulets and were probably mumbling prayers and promises to their own deities right now. He heard the nervous shuffling of feet around him and then a sharp intake of breath from the young lad Erik as a stone whistled past him. Holding his scythe ever more firmly, Erik's eyes darted towards the spikes that he had got the village blacksmith to weld on to the farming tool, transforming it into a weapon. From the look in his eyes, Caedmon knew that Erik's fear now was that somebody had noticed his momentary lapse. Caedmon turned his head to see a stone hurtling towards him and raised his shield just in time.

As he lowered his shield, Caedmon's heart lurched as he saw the Vikings rushing towards him. He knew that they intended to intimidate and terrify, and they were doing it well. In the fear and excitement, he noticed the way that their clothing rippled behind them, axes and swords gleaming in the moonlight, and saw one huge warrior, built like a stone altar, that he would do his best to avoid. This was the moment when time slowed down and a man could be overwhelmed by his fear of what lay ahead. And yet there was also the excitement and fever of battle.

He picked his first opponent and, with a roar, pursued him. The young man turned to confront him and Caedmon used his sword to pummel at his opponent's shield. Then, when he saw the shield begin to give way, Caedmon swung his sword round, slicing through his opponent's tendons. The man lay exposed and stunned on the ground. Bringing his sword down, Caedmon killed him quickly and looked round to find his next man to challenge. It was always better to be the challenger than the challenged.

In the chaos of battle, he glanced around every so often to locate his friends. Caught up in the unworldly and febrile atmosphere, their faces shone with fear or he could not see them at all. Thin and sinewy, Caedmon chose his confrontations in seconds but wisely. At first he hawked after the weak and inexperienced, giving them a quick end. As the battle progressed, the hand-to-hand fighting became more difficult. He duelled with men who had

trained as much as he had and anticipated his every move, but eventually they would make a wrong move and he hoped that he despatched them to Valhalla quickly. He was bruised, bloody and cut when he saw Ælfric – forever seeking out trouble – begin to duel with the huge man, with muscles like stone.

Fearful for his friend, he forgot the pain from his wounds. An intense feeling of fury that must have been given to him by the gods overwhelmed him. He had to reach Ælfric and the Viking; everything else seemed small and diminished. With a roar he charged toward the pair. A couple of challengers stepped toward him but with a skill and athleticism that he did not know he had, he knocked them aside. Each challenger fell by the wayside, bewildered by the speed and the accuracy with which he bought down his sword and then carried apace. Running towards Ælfric and the mammoth Viking, Caedmon seemed to have an awareness of every fold, every stretch and every hammering that the sword he grasped had ever received. When he reached the pair it was clear that Ælfric – always living on the edge – was out of his depth this time. Caedmon shouldered his friend out of the way and squared up to the Viking.

The man was clearly a chief, a ruthless, experienced killer. Yet Caedmon was overtaken by a frenzied fury. Onlookers would later say how he seemed to grow – the energy and fury now showing in his face, which glowed as if he had eaten hot coals. He bit his sword and howled like a wolf. Neither fire nor iron could harm him. They saw that he was capable of hurting friend or foe.

Caedmon no longer knew his limits. If God or the gods wished him to fight this man, then he was not a coward. The unknown warrior was in front of him brandishing his iron sword but Caedmon felt absolutely fearless.

The unthinking rage started to settle and a cool ruthlessness took over. Opposite him, the Viking warrior took a deep breath, his eyes blazing at Caedmon through his helmet. Yet the Viking seemed to be waiting for Caedmon to attack. This was an old trick and Caedmon replied with one of his own. He ran at the Viking before attempting to slash at one of his weak points. Then Caedmon retreated. He could hear the sound of a sword slicing through the air as his adversary anticipated him.

His foe did not waste any energy on pointless stabs towards his stomach or chest. Instead he harried him constantly. The Viking's sword cut through the air with speed and grace. They lunged and parried and when Caedmon weakened he had to dodge a well-aimed thrust towards his neck or under his arms. He lived moment by moment, protecting himself from the blows and mesmerised by how the sword had become an instrument of exquisite beauty and fear. He was not instantly aware that the killer jab had been delivered until his legs weakened beneath him and he collapsed.

The Viking stood above him. He paused for a second as he raised his sword up, maybe thanking a Norse God. Looking up, Caedmon realised that many men must have seen him the way that he was seeing this mighty Viking now. Had they thought about the world that they were leaving in these last moments? The colours of the night sky were all the more lustrous for being the last glimpse Caedmon would have of them. He would not leave this world in fear but rejoicing in it. Especially when the Viking had the effrontery to pause to mumble a prayer. Such arrogance deserved retribution. With a surge of energy that he had not expected, Caedmon rolled on to his back and, like a long-limbed hare, he sprung upwards, his legs thumped into the Viking's chest. Caedmon heard the Viking land on the ground and bones crack.

They lay exhausted and injured. Both taken for dead, with the battle raging around them. Unable to think about what was happening around him, Caedmon closed his eyes. The voices gradually became fainter and fainter, and he was aware that he might well have little time left. He was woken by a burning sensation in his breast. Swallowing his pain, he could hear the other man moaning. As time progresses he could see birds of prey starting to circle above them. He did not hate the Viking who had taken his life. Both of them were brave warriors. They had done what they had to do for their own kin. The fact that neither had been able to kill the other showed that they had met their equal. Neither was the stronger. Maybe they had both brought retribution from the gods or God for the other. But they had both fought bravely. He would go on to meet his God, although he hoped that some of the minor gods and goddesses would be there, maybe as saints. He suspected that the Viking would go to his Valhalla.

He heard a sharp cry of pain, barely suppressed by the Viking, and impulsively moved his hand on to the man's shoulder and squeezed it. When the man's arm moved, Caedmon flinched – seemingly the kindness was rebuffed. Then the arm moved again and he felt a reassuring hand touch his own shoulder.

They died together. The Vikings believed that magic was used both in the making and the using of the sword, and that some of the wielder's soul was shared with the blade. It was only right, therefore to bury the sword with the Viking. Later the sword that Caedmon had used was removed from the battle scene, it was a weapon lent by his lord after all. But, as recognition of his bravery, Caedmon was buried with his shield, which was made in the style of the Anglo-Saxons.

In the months to come, Caedmon's possessions were shared amongst relatives. His mother heard news that the Vikings had been pushed back at Tempsford, bringing a sense of security back to Beda's Ford. She found the grieving hardest at festival times. He had always been ready to check on the animals, making sure they were warm enough and had enough feed. She expected a brief blast of cold air as he ran in to join the feast, with all the assembled family turning round in mock condemnation. His plate and his drinking cup were passed to her. She knew which was his from the patterns and, unknown to his father, recognised the day of his death using the cup and praying to one of the old pagan gods. She continued the ritual until she became too old to raise her hands to drink without help. Sitting in a corner with her elderly hands quivering around the curves of the cup, she remembered her son with both love and pride.

This story is based on a sword found in Russell Park in the nineteenth century by the Reverend Wyatt and now part of the collection of The Higgins museum in Bedford. From the *Anglo-Saxon Chronicles*, Wyatt already knew of a Viking raid in the tenth century. When he found the Viking sword he was convinced that he had found the site of a battle, or at the very least an intensely violent scuffle. However, the lack of excavationary rigour that was part of the life of a Victorian antiquarian means that today archaeologists have no clear evidence pointing to a battle there. Instead the Reverend Wyatt may have been rooting around in the remnants of an Anglo-Saxon burial site. Intriguingly, the Viking sword, with its iron handle – rather than the wooden and leather pommel that Anglo-Saxons used – is very unusual at such burial sites.

In my mind's eye, I always picture the sword polished and with the edges sharpened ready for battle. It is a tantalising and teasing glimpse of a warrior's life many centuries ago and well worth a visit to The Higgins museum to see.

5

A TRUE TALE

The Romany woman was picking bluebells by the lane when she saw it. It looked like a long worm and she could see the tip of something white wriggling and writhing before it disappeared into the ground. She scanned the landscape with her eyes until she saw a flicker of movement in the line of trees by the edge of the wood a mile off. Deep in Gypsy lore she knew that this was a dragon, one with no wings, more like a serpent to those who were not adept in the old ways.

It was a dragon, nonetheless. It had emptied the country and now it was hungry again, craving flesh to fill its belly. Hoping to deceive the unwary, it had buried itself under the soil except the tips of its tail in the lane and its head in the wood. Luckily such cunning had not deceived the woman.

The Romany woman continued to stand in the lane overseeing the field. She expected to be alone in the lane as it was an ancient trackway that few knew of. Consequently, she was bemused to hear a noise not too far away. As the sound grew louder, however, it became more strident and less human. By the time her ears had become accustomed to the sound of gobbling, she was not surprised to see twenty geese waddling down the lane.

The woman looked on as one of the geese paddled over to the tail of the long worm-like dragon. Curious, it shifted its head to one side and gazed at the tail. Lurching forward, it pecked at the tail. As the dragon's tail writhed, the goose pecked staccato-style, clouds of dust rising. Catching the dragon's tail in the vice-like grip of its beak, the goose tugged and tugged. Then all the other geese formed a line and pulled with the goose and they tugged and they tugged.

The woman ran to safety when she saw the ground between the lane and the woods trembling as the dragon tried to free itself. The earth shook with a tremor as its tail hit the ground and the geese scattered in all directions. As the dragon reared its head, the geese started to panic. The dragon rose and the geese, not looking where they were going, careered into one another. Overshadowed by the vast bulk of the dragon, the geese trampled over one another in their haste to escape. The dragon turned its head toward them and, with one sweep of its neck, ate up all of the geese. It ate so much that it fell asleep where it was, nestling its head on top of its scaly shoulders and leaving the gold that it had hidden in its nest for all to see.

All the while, the woman had been hiding. Now she stepped out from the shadows. She looked round furtively, ignoring the rumbling from the dragon's stomach. Then she cut across to the nest, hungrily scanning the landscape as she slipped the gold into her coat. When the dragon woke up, it ran amok looking for its missing gold; farmers would gladly have returned the gold but they never found out where it had gone. The Romany woman, meanwhile, enjoyed spending the dragon's gold and she was generous to her family. For a time, you could always spot one of her relatives. They always had gold teeth and gold jewellery and were renowned for their wit and bravery wherever they went.

6

YOUNG SUSAN

Susan opened the door, stepping out of the ballroom and into the dark hallway. She was dressed for dancing. However, her dress was plain and to a fashionable eye it was obvious that she needed to make do and mend. She gazed up at the staircase, comparing it to the grandly carved staircase of Houghton House of Ampthill. Houghton House was the country seat of her aunt and uncle, and rather grand. She had been sent there to help her to make connections and make a good marriage. At first her cousins had found her amusing. She had wandered from room to room, so obviously overwhelmed by the spacious extravagant rooms. They laughed when they found her inspecting the finely carved furniture and she had often been seen running her hands along the figures above the staircase with something like awe. Now they barely noticed her and treated her as something in between a servant and a young sister.

She frowned, her thoughts returning to the ball. She ought to be grateful that her cousins had brought her to this ball. She must return to it or she would appear ungrateful. Standing in this hallway had been like a breath of fresh air but now she must re-enter the fray. Susan squeezed through the crowds and was approached by the local vicar. She stood transfixed as the tall kingfisher of a man talked relentlessly. Like waves reaching a beach, as soon as one sentence broke, then another and another followed. Eventually, breaking eye contact for just a second, Susan saw her chance. Her cousin Anne had beckoned to her to come over. She quickly sidestepped to one side, murmuring her excuse. When she reached her cousin, she was instructed to fetch another shawl. Showing a recklessness that was completely out of character, Susan took this as an instruction to return to Houghton Hall for the garment, dashing out of the hall toward the yard.

She flicked the reins to encourage the horse. As she did so she shook her head ruefully, unable to explain what had overcome her. She was not nervous driving the horse trap, despite the late hour. Instead she felt liberated from the stultifying atmosphere of the ball. The trees overhanging Ampthill Road meant that there was little light, but the horses knew their way back to Houghton House. From there she would pick up her cousin's favourite shawl, grateful to have some time away from the crowds. She knew Anne was spoilt but she was actually the easiest relative to like and Susan could rely on her to explain away her own present behaviour. Glancing over her shoulder, Susan could see the light of another carriage behind her, this one had a lantern to light the way. Maybe it was someone else trying to escape the ball.

She was jolted from her thoughts when she suddenly heard a sound and saw that the other carriage was now mere yards away. Susan thought that she would find a way of pulling over to the side of the road to allow it to pass. There was a shout from behind and looking round, she was horrified to see the other horses racing towards her, the driver flicking the whip.

Susan reacted quickly, leaning forward as she urged on her horses, convinced that the other driver was coping with horses freaked by a small animal or similar. Waiting for the driver to slow his horse down, she cast a glance over her shoulder several times. Still the other carriage clung closely to her path, the driver shifting forward and shouting. However much the road twisted and turned, the carriage did not slow.

As they climbed up the hill, the rattling on the pony trap became more of a slow clattering. She shot a look over her shoulder and could just make out the grim look upon the face of the driver behind her. Both of her horses were struggling as they laboured up the slope but she felt sorry for the horse that was pulling the carriage behind her – it's mouth foaming from the rough treatment that it had received. What did this sinister figure want from her? She stared intently at the road. He mustn't catch her. If he showed such violence to his horses, she dared not think what he would do to a woman on her own with the darkness enveloping them. They reached the top of the hill and she raced towards Houghton House. With a crack of the whip, she spared a thought for her family who had sent her so far away. Then she drove as if she had become one with the road, reacting to every curve and slight kink in the road.

Finally, she swerved into the grounds of Houghton House. She could not see the house yet, but with all of the family at the ball, she knew it would be quiet. The only sound was that of the horses' hooves beating as the carriage cut a swathe through the grounds. The world diminished to the grounds, the house and the two vehicles approaching. Nothing else mattered.

Onward Susan rode, past the grand entrance to the country house and towards the servants' entrance, where she had a chance of summoning help quickly. She swerved to a stop, the horses staggering as she jumped off the pony trap. Susan pelted towards the servants' entrance, panting. On reaching the doorway, she began to turn round, hoping to lock the door and call the servants for help. All of a sudden her whole world lurched sideways and she shrieked as her head cracked against the doorway. Everything was very confused now. Two figures were grappling with one another on the ground. She cried out, recognising the footman from a neighbouring house. She couldn't see the features of the other man but she did see his shiny black shoes kick out and heard the footman groan. The stranger stood up and reached inside his jacket. Everything slowed down now as Susan realised what was happening. There was a silver arc and a slashing noise. Uncomprehending, her mind tried to link the noise with something ordinary – a knife cutting through butter or scissors ripping through silk. Then there was an eerie silence, broken by the sound of whimpering from the man lying on the ground. Stepping over the wounded body, the stranger rounded on her. Suddenly, a noise from the back of the servants' hall was transformed into the thundering of feet. Flattening herself against the door, Susan watched as a multitude of servants wrestled the stranger to the ground. One servant stayed behind with the footman and the others took the stranger away. The housekeeper came out with a bowl full of hot water and strips of sheets torn into bandages. She hunched over the body. Her head hovered above the footman's head and she seemed to be listening intently. Then abruptly her shoulders descended and the woman lost her sense of urgency. She gestured with a nod at the young men surrounding her. They returned with blankets and gently shepherded Susan away.

The doctor visited and Susan was told by him to rest for the next couple of weeks. It was only when she felt strong enough that her cousin Anne sat on the edge of her bed and told her what had really happened. The footman driving the carriage had been sent to fetch a bag for one of the ladies from a neighbouring house. As he pulled up closer to Susan's pony trap, he had seen a figure raise himself up from the back of the pony trap. The figure, with his knife poised ready to strike her, was only deterred when the footman began to shout at her. Forgetting his own safety, the footman rode through the countryside, determined to warn her of the danger that she was in. When they reached the servants' entrance, he saw the pony trap stop. He saw Susan running towards the servants' entrance and seconds later he saw the man leap out of the back of her carriage and attempted to seize her. The footman ran towards the servants' entrance, focused on keeping her safe. When he saw that the stranger's hand was outstretched and his fingertips were almost touching her clothing, he threw himself at the other figure, catching his legs and toppling him to the floor. As Susan knew, the footman was

never to recover from the fight, but he was able to whisper to the housekeeper what had happened before he died.

It is not known for sure what the mysterious man's intentions were – to assault or steal from Susan – but the story of the attempted attack spread like wildfire through Bedfordshire. In Susan's lifetime the house was always associated with the tale. Like ripples on a pond after throwing a stone, there is still an effect, even when nothing can be seen on the surface, and even now the land and the house are imprinted with the memory of that frightening scene. That is why the ruins of this once proud house still ring with the sound of galloping horses and there have been sightings of shadowy figures that quickly vanish if challenged.

Today Houghton House is a ruined house on the ridge near Ampthill in the middle of what were once splendid grounds but is now mostly farmland. Built with orange-red bricks and Totternhoe stone, it inspired the 'House Beautiful' in John Bunyan's *Pilgrim's Progress* and gives a fine view from the ridge on to the surrounding countryside. On visiting the ruins, you can see the outline of the grand entrance and trace the steps of the ceremonial route between the hall and the Great Chamber. Walking through the now empty rooms you can imagine servants bustling through the panelled hall, smoking room, parlour and library. The staircase that once graced the hall of Houghton House now adorns the Swan Hotel in Bedford.

7

THE LITTLE
BLUE MAN

Alex, Tony, Kerry, Andrew, Colin and John were all aged ten years old and were happily playing on Studham Common on their way to afternoon school. John was boasting about his dad's new Ford Anglia, although the rest of the group had grown tired of the talk of the Italian styling. Instead, their minds were full of *Doctor Who*. He had just gone through his first regeneration and now Patrick Troughton played the part.

Only five miles from Luton, they were walking through a haven for wildlife. The Common positively teemed with life. As the children strolled along, they passed by a hedgerow that had been growing on that spot since the Middle Ages. The ancient hedgerow was home to dormice and a rich larder for many species. Whilst chatting to each other, their fingers may have brushed past a variety of wildflowers, their feet stamping on a miscellany of insects and waving away unusual species of butterflies.

They were in the Dell, a shallow valley thickly strewn with hawthorn, gorse and bracken, which they scrambled or tunnelled their way through. The injunctions from their parents to keep their school uniforms clean were forgotten. Their hair was snagged by the bushes, their faces rosy with excitement and their trousers sodden at the knees, the hems glistening with mud.

The children began to climb the slight bank out of the valley to arrive at school slightly breathless but content. Colin was at the back of the line. In his mind, he had taken the dangerous role of protecting the rear and turning round he scanned the landscape for an imaginary foe, hidden but lethal. His friends were all ahead of him so when Colin saw something, the rest of the children were only half-aware of him stopping mid-sentence and then gasping. Then he started shouting.

He was shouting and pointing to the bank on the other side of the Dell. There, a short distance away, was a little blue man with a helmet and a beard. 'Look!' Colin exclaimed and the children charged along their side of the bank, squinting in order to comprehend the figure on the other ridge of the valley. All of a sudden there was a puff of smoke, and when it had dissipated, there was no sight of the man.

Aware that they had seen something very unusual, the atmosphere was now highly charged with excitement. 'Where did he go?!' one of the group cried, and they ran along the bottom of the Dell, searching in earnest for the elusive man. He appeared again, on the other side of the valley to where Colin had first spotted him. The group hurtled toward him, not heeding how they would stop if they reached him, but again there was a puff of smoke. The little blue man seemed to have melted into the scenery and, although they reached the spot in a matter of seconds, nobody could find him anywhere nearby.

They were all looking for their quarry now, shouting orders and suggestions to each other. They broke into two groups, one on each side of the valley. There was a glimpse of blue on the bank where he had originally been seen and one group set off in pursuit. Looking for him through the bushes, they became aware of voices, a continuous and incomprehensible babble in another language. Now they became wary, as they feared that the little blue man was talking to other blue men and calling for assistance.

The next time the little blue man appeared, they did not rush towards him as they had done previously, despite their curiosity and the thousands of repressed questions bursting inside them. With gentle steps, they made their way to the top of the Dell and circled the spot where they had last seen him. This time he didn't disappear but remained where he was, standing motionless. Uncertain what to do next, the children milled around dithering until one of the group suggested that they run to school and tell their teacher.

Miss Newcomb thought she was about to disappear under an avalanche of excited children. 'You won't believe it, miss,' was the phrase she heard most often in the incoherent, tumbling, sometimes stuttering, onslaught of words. Small and slight, with light brown hair and glasses, she was a stickler for routine and lavish with praise. She thought precisely and logically about many things, including her teaching. All of the children in front of her adored her and wanted to impress her.

The children paused when she started to speak. They reminded her of puppies waiting for a chocolate treat, their faces intently focused on what she was saying. 'Now. I want you to speak one at a time, starting with Alex and tell me what happened.' But it was no use, as soon as Alex started to tell his side of the story, the other children couldn't contain their impatience.

'Children,' said Miss Newcomb quietly and that was their cue to stop abruptly. Their eyes were eager and entreating and she knew that if she gave one child the chance to speak then their excitement would well up all over again. When she asked them to sit down without speaking to one another and write their account of what had happened, they did so without question.

The accounts agreed that the man was tall by comparison with themselves but part of that height was accounted for by a huge two-foot helmet. All described the man as blue and, when asked further, the children said that it was a greyish blue. Through the helmet they could see a fringe of hair, two round eyes and a small triangle in the place of a nose. He had worn a one-piece tunic with a broad black belt wrapped around it. Hooked on to the belt at the front was a black box about six inches square. The arms were short and were held straight down close to the sides at all times. The legs and feet were indistinct. His beard was full and divided at his chin, with the two sides running as far down as his chest.

Believers in UFOs seized on the children's' accounts, they felt that the long beard the children had described was actually breathing apparatus, the box hooked on to his belt was a communicator with a spaceship and the puff of smoke was ionizing radiation. Sceptics responded with scientific explanations, including St Elmo's Fire to explain the little man's blue-coloured skin. St Elmo's fire can be produced after a thunderstorm from plasma that glows bright blue or violet and looks like fire. Although it usually appears around church spires and other tall pointed structures, it has also been seen at a lower level on grass and trees.

The children remained steadfast with their story. Local newspapers, including the *Dunstable Gazette*, were interested in what had happened on the Common. The children kept to the description that they had given just minutes after the incident and were supported by their teacher. This was no ordinary fairy tale nor was it an obvious figment of the children's imaginations, especially with descriptions so similar. Nobody who knew the children disputed that something had really happened, but what actually transpired remains a mystery to this day.

8

TILL I SEE YOU AGAIN

The cheery-faced woman of Barton-le-Clay lived a meagre existence. Now we might call it dire poverty, regularly going to sleep with the ache of hunger in her belly, clothes so worn that they did little more than hide her thin form and certainly didn't keep her warm. Yet Agnes considered herself rich, because somehow, despite the winters in which she had only just escaped starvation, she had brought up two sons. Jeck, aged twelve, and Hugh, aged ten, cherished their mother and she felt that they were worth all the sacrifices she had made. The two sons had never taken to schoolwork and they found farm work dull. They could see a life ahead of them with each day much the same as the one before. What's more, their mother was so frail it looked as if a gust of wind would knock her over and one bad winter would break her health for good.

Agnes earned some money straw plaiting. The boys farmed during the day but during the late evening and night they always explored the woods. One evening Jeck and Hugh were playing a game of hide-and-seek in the woods. Jeck, the fair-haired brother was able to lie down completely quiet, without alerting any of the wildlife to his presence. As he was hiding, a rabbit popped its head up through a rabbit hole. Jeck watched it for a moment and then, quick as a flash, he grabbed it by the ears, abandoning the game of hide and seek with a cry of delight. As country boys, they knew how to kill and skin a rabbit. The gnawing hunger in their belly overrode all worries that the rabbit belonged to the landowner. It was as they were picking the last of the meat off the bone that both brothers started to voice the idea that was in their heads. They could easily knit small nets to place over the rabbit warrens and, with their knowledge of the countryside and their quick reactions, they would be able to see off starvation.

They worked in the fields for a tenant farmer who rented the land from a member of the aristocracy. The poaching began in a small way, with some hours in the woods after working in the field, and they caught enough rabbits to ensure that they and their mother had sufficient food. However, the long evenings meant that the two boys grew more and more tired. Nevertheless, they found that by leaving a rabbit by the kitchen door of the tenant farmer then nothing was said if, occasionally, they were too tired to turn up for work. As they grew more experienced and more skilled, they sold the odd rabbit and saved up enough money to buy large nets.

Now they were able to use the large nets to work the meadows, stealing out late at night when they were less likely to be seen. This work could not be done alone – one brother was needed to work the net and send the ferrets in to hunt the rabbits, and one to run a beating line round the field to shoo the rabbits into the net. Whoever had the job of walking the fields found that everything looked different at that time of night. There was many a time when

Jeck or Hugh found their imagination working overtime. A bush would take on the shape of a gamekeeper and the best solution was to close their eyes and quieten their mind until it became a bush again.

One night, as Hugh was casting the net, he began to feel as though there was someone breathing heavily behind him. The brothers were always conscious of the need to work quickly and the likelihood that gamekeepers would find them if they took a long time. So he tried to repress the thought and continued with the process of gathering sections of the net and throwing them over the field. Still the feeling continued and it was becoming more and more real; not only could he feel the breath on his neck but there was the distinct sound of grinding teeth. When he could take it no longer, he looked around and saw a cow less than a foot away from his backside. The cow looked intently at Hugh as he skittered halfway across the field in fright. It ambled away as Hugh tried to calm himself down, but a few minutes later it was back again and this time Hugh grabbed a stick and, walloping it repeatedly on the backside, shooed it away. Having made enough noise to wake the dead, let alone the tenant farmer and the gamekeeper, the brothers gave up for the night.

By now Jeck had reached thirteen and Hugh was eleven years old. As they grew up, their night-time existence became the focus of their life. There were stories of close shaves with the gamekeepers looking for them whilst they were sitting in a tree above them, falling asleep exhausted in a hayrick and waking up to find rats licking apple juice from their fingers, and long walks home because they were scared of an enormous bull. They always needed to be aware of the risk of gamekeepers and the gangs of poachers working in the area. However, they made few enemies. They would always help out another family that was struggling as much as they once had. Just when a family had reconciled themselves to moving to the work-house, families would wake to find the body of a rabbit on their doorstep. Moreover, as they worked a small area, the big gangs of poachers tended to leave the brothers alone.

When Jeck reached sixteen they experimented with shooting larger animals. They bought a rifle, failing to ask why the larger gangs had not wanted such a weapon. Together they headed into the woods, creeping through the trees until they came upon a group of three deer. Two older deer stood nibbling at the undergrowth with a single fawn nearby. Jeck was careful to point the rifle at one of the older ones, pulled the trigger and jumped as the charge exploded. The rifle flew into the air, firing off and shot down the young deer. The pair were horrified to have killed the youngster as it seemed wrong to kill a fawn before it had reached its prime, but worse was to come.

The young deer had been the pet of the lord's youngest daughter and when it was discovered to be missing the poachers were blamed. Moreover, the lord let it be known that there would be transportation for whoever was found with it. The body of the deer was moved from one farm labourer's house to another, each of them scared of being found out but willing to help the two boys who had helped others close to starvation. On Christmas Eve, all of the locals were gathered in the church. The candles cast long dappled shadows over the nave of the church, whilst the farm labourers and their families clustered around the nativity scene could see each other's rosy faces glowing in the tallowed light. The priest may not have been so happy with his nativity scene if he had looked further. Whilst gamekeepers searched houses, anxious to please their master, rolled up in a blanket and rocked in the cradle was the body of the baby deer.

When the landowner died and his eldest son became lord then life became much tougher for poachers. He was ruthless, putting pressure on the Justice of the Peace to give long periods of imprisonment to those found poaching and laying mantraps to break legs or even kill poachers. Soon the gangs of poachers had lost men and they were insistent that the brothers join forces with them. The brothers – wary of the gangs, who were often ruthless and violent – found a compromise by working over a smaller area but their chances of getting caught were steadily becoming greater. Their mother, Agnes, pleaded with her sons to give up. When she woke up in the early hours of the morning and saw that their bedding was untouched, she foresaw capture followed quickly by imprisonment and death. On their return she argued that she would take in more straw plaiting. Anything to make them give up poaching.

One night, the two boys, worried by stories of gamekeepers in the meadows, had returned to their old haunt of the woods and had set up nets over rabbit holes to catch rabbits as they left their warren. They still knew every path, every tree and every mound. So when Hugh heard the sound of a branch cracking, there was no hesitation in sprinting towards the nearest meadow. Unfortunately, he was unaware that the gamekeepers had dug a deep pit, covering it with branches and vegetation as camouflage, and he tumbled down the side of the pit, breaking his ankle. He summoned his brother with the birdcall that they used as a joint signal.

Jeck tried to find branches long enough to give Hugh something to hold on to so he could pull himself out. From inside the pit, the younger brother could hear the sound of his brother fumbling around in the undergrowth looking for something to help him. Intense periods of activity were followed by silence and he could imagine Jeck's despair. He softly called to Jeck to leave him, as long as one of them was alive to look after his mother. Their eyes met as Jeck peered into the pit. As dawn broke, the elder brother was found by gamekeepers sitting by the side of the hole, waiting for them. The brothers were determined to stay together. They hoped their mother would be taken in and cared for.

The gamekeepers were delighted to find not one poacher but two. As meek as lambs, the two boys were led off, the younger brother leaning on his older brother to avoid putting weight on his ankle. If the keepers were expecting a fight, they didn't get one.

The long slow walk to a stable in the big house where the boys were locked up gave everyone time to think. The boys had no sureties. They had made little money from poaching, preferring to help those around them instead.

In the next Bedfordshire Quarter Sessions, the charge was read to the court: 'On the 13th day of September at Barton-le-Clay in the said county, these men did feloniously attempt to steal livestock contrary to the form of the statute in such case made and provided.' The gamekeepers were asked to appear, stating their name and occupation, and described their discovery of the two young men who now stood quiet and subdued before the court. The judge was aware that the boys had no criminal record. They were not part of the gangs of poachers who were well known in the area. He could not set them free yet he did not want to send them to Bedford Gaol. Typhus was uncontrollable in the prison and these two boys might not last more than a couple of weeks.

He asked them to stand. 'This crime is an offence against the game law. You have said little but we cannot let you continue, shamelessly flouting the law and stealing his lordship's property. You have already pleaded guilty to the case brought against you today, but in light of the evidence given, do you have anything to say?' Both boys mumbled, 'I have nothing to say'. There was a gasp in the court as the judge gave the sentence of transportation. As they left the court, Agnes stormed towards them. Months of anxiety were unleashed. Spitting out each word, they seemed to shrink as she towered over them. Had they not heard how she wanted them to give up poaching? Well it served them right that they were being sent to Australia. Don't come back, she told them forcefully.

In the days, months and years to come, Agnes would replay this scene in her mind. Would they now feel that not only did she not love them but that she had never loved them? What memory would they have of her now? What fury had overtaken her? Yet she had heard in songs and folk tales of people who had escaped

transportation and returned. Careless of her own needs, she feared for them and did not want them to return and face further punishment for their escape. She hoped that she had convinced the boys that she would never give them a warm welcome if they tried to return, but maybe she had taken it too far. She thought that if it took those moments to keep her boys alive and with a chance of making a good life in Australia, then maybe it was worth it.

After that Agnes, although neighbours tried to make sure she never went hungry, aged quickly. Within weeks her hair was completely grey and where her face had been lined, she now looked grey and wrinkled. When she spoke, she spoke of the long journey across the sea that her boys would be taking. Her eyes were clear and her speech was not confused, but the look in her eye showed that she wanted to be far away and she mumbled words of love: 'Till I see you again, my boys, Till I see you again.' Months and months of dwelling on what her boys would be doing took their toll and she took to wandering the fields day and night. She clearly imagined both a watery grave at sea and a prosperous new life for her boys and, with these conflicting thoughts, she was forever restless, unable to be sure of their fate. She became known as the mad woman of Barton, a wet bedraggled figure shaking her fists at the wind, howling and raving, laughing and crying. She had meant the final act in the court as an act of kindness, but now she was trapped in her own mind.

It was seen as a final release when Agnes' remains were found in the waters near the mill. Neighbours came and collected her poor emaciated body from the reeds. The wind was wailing like a banshee as they carefully lifted her up and the reeds bowed like supplicants as they carried her away. The end of her life had been difficult for all to watch and her body had suffered as much as her mind. She was not forgotten, however, as in the years since her death she has been seen at the mill beckoning others to follow her into the waters surrounding the mill. Most recently, a former owner of the mill reported encounters with an old lady, notable for her long grey hair, who waved a bony finger at him, motioning for him to follow. He never did.

9

THE MATCHMAKER

Tom was a hard-working man who made bowstrings in Henlow. He had learnt his art from his father and his father spent many a long hour teaching him how to get the tension just right on the bowstring. It was so exacting that young Tom did not get out very much. He had just one friend in the village and that was Mary. They didn't talk about much but they would go to a nearby lake and skim stones before climbing trees or discussing setting up the jig he used to make the strings. Tom was proud of his craft and he knew that it was important in the wars against the French. He was a quiet child and then a quiet man. As he grew up, he knew that if he wanted to talk, Mary would listen.

As Tom and Mary got older, a number of men would go walking out with Mary for a while but they never walked out with her for long. And as for Tom, he was too awkward to approach women and dreaded the idea of making conversation with someone he did not know well. When he was twenty, Tom's father introduced him to a matchmaker and told him that she would find a wife for him. Tom, usually quiet, insisted that he meet women outside of his village and was emphatic that he would not marry a woman that did not meet with the approval of Mary. The matchmaker shrugged pragmatically. If the young man wanted to bring along a girl who was like a sister to him, then who was she to stand in his way. He was also very attractive. She was certain the combination of ruggedly handsome and shyness would mean that he would be married within a week.

First they travelled to Kempston to meet Jane, who was a basket weaver. Jane was blond and curvy, with the brightest smile Tom had ever seen. Buffeted by soft winds, she showed him how to weave a basket. As she created a cross with the willow and then gradually added more willow to create a base, her hands tentatively brushed his and she looked up, smiling gently into his eyes. There was the immediate rapport of two people who were both artisans and who took great joy in their work. They worked quietly away for an hour or more enjoying each other's company.

On finishing a basket, Jane gently levered herself to stand up and collect more willow but she staggered and fell into Tom's arms. 'Oh Tom,' she said, 'you take my breath away.' Tom was worried – first she fell over unexpectedly and now she was telling him that she was unable to breathe. He could not remember how to look after someone with such problems with their health but he did know how he had seen his neighbours dealing with children who had trouble breathing. So with great speed he pushed Jane on the shoulder, twisting her round so that she was lying head-down on his lap and, using the heel of his hand, inflicted several sharp blows to her back. Later he could not understand why, despite saving her life, she did not want to see him again. Mary told him not to worry. They would both have been too involved with their work to get on.

Next they travelled to Luton to meet Mae, who was a hat maker. Mae spent her day making straw hats. A tall and willowy brunette, she looked like a breath of wind would knock her over but, when she told Tom about herself, she made it clear that she worked hard and would be pleased to marry in order to escape the work. As she fashioned a jaunty straw hat, she told him of her dreams of visiting other places, maybe somewhere as far away as London. 'Oh Tom,' she breathed, 'take me on a whole new adventure with you.' While Tom considered this idea, however, she suddenly exclaimed, 'Oh dear, I seem to have something in my eye!'

Tom did not waste any time, he knew that eyesight could be damaged quickly and a small piece of straw could be dislodged with water. With great speed he pushed three of Mae's sisters aside in his rush to reach the well. Unfortunately, the smallest vessel he could find was a bucket but he filled it up anyway and wove back past her sisters, who were nursing cuts and bruises, to reach Mae. She looked surprised as he threw the bucket of water into her face. Later he could not understand why the sight problems she had referred to no longer seemed to exist. Furthermore, she had left clear instructions that she never wanted to see him again. Mary told him not to worry, Mae had been too keen on going to London and he would never be happy leaving his hometown.

The matchmaker was starting to see that Tom was no ordinary match, so she sent him to visit a group of women who worked on the rivers. The roads in this region were rutted and notoriously difficult for moving heavy goods, and so the rivers were often used for more unmanageable goods. This meant that the river workers were very strong as they were used to lugging sacks. What is more, they were very brave, as some sections of the river were dangerous and almost unnavigable. She felt that these women were more direct about what they wanted and would not say anything that Tom would misunderstand. When Mary and Tom reached their destination next to the water, the air carried the earthy smell of soil from crops. The men wore waistcoats and had rolled up their sleeves ready to move heavy boxes from one boat to another. Despite the presence of these burly river men, Tom still stood out with his rugged good looks and, as he arrived, the women gave him looks that clearly said that if marriage was not on the cards then something else was. But Tom was oblivious. One of the matriarchs took him to one side and started to ask him about himself. Tom was soon deep into an explanation of the setting of his jig used in bow-making and held up his arms to demonstrate the tension needed in a bow-string. The matriarch was not a demonstrative woman – in fact she was quiet and respectable – but Tom standing in front of her like that, diffident and handsome, was a like a work of art and she couldn't resist reaching up to touch his muscles the way that she would reach out towards a statue. Her husband, glancing towards her, was immediately stung by jealousy.

The husband finished his conversation abruptly and strode over to them. Standing almost directly in between Tom and his wife, he demanded to know what was going on. Not satisfied with his wife's explanation of bowstrings or some such nonsense, he insisted that the young man join him for a drink and some arm-wrestling. Soon a group of mainly young women were huddled around the two men. Some oil was passed around for the men to massage their muscles, but more care seemed to be taken to make sure that Tom was well prepared. A space was prepared for the competition and the men stared directly at one another as their arms entwined and their palms met. On the count of three, Tom attempted to explain how his worth as a human being could not be measured by this competition and was surprised to find that in the distraction he had pushed his competitor's arm to the ground. Tom was raised into the air as the winner and borne away to celebrate while his erstwhile competitor was comforted by his wife.

As Tom was lowered carefully on to the ground, he could see men and women reaching for pipes and drums. One started to play a tune and others followed. As the melody evolved, one of the women leapt into the space cleared by Tom's arrival. Others joined in the playing, leaving to take a gulp of ale and then rejoining, as more and more of the water workers joined in the celebration. Tom, looking on, could see the happiness of this community but knew that it was not for him. His happiness was based on quietness with someone special to him and at the moment it was further away from him than ever. He crept away quietly.

A day later Mary found him looking over the lake at Henlow. Tom's eyes were moving restlessly across the lake, finding a reflection of his sadness. He did not wish to upset his father, who wanted him to marry, but he was resigned to not finding a match. Mary picked up a stone and placed it in Tom's hands, and together they skimmed stones as it grew darker. Tom found that the melancholy shared became much easier to bear. Mary nudged Tom's shoulder with her own and said, 'Let's go and see that matchmaker'.

When the two of them turned up the next day, the matchmaker took a long look at the two of them. 'As you know,' she said, 'I am a wise woman. I understand the herbs to use if a woman is in childbirth or if you or your animals are taken ill. My family have a knowledge of the earth going back generations. If I wanted, I could make spells to make you a lord, to curse or to blight your crops, but I cannot make you see what is in front of you. Mary, you may feel that you want excitement and wish to leave but you seem to feel happiest when you are lost in the silence of the landscape. Tom, forget your family, think of the person whose approval you seek most and marry them.' And Tom and Mary looked at each other as if for the first time.

10

The Dunstable Swan Jewel

The story goes, then, that the young Lord William in Dunstable was out hunting. He was usually a kind young man, and would listen carefully to any tales of injustice that were brought to him, deducing who was exaggerating the most and who had the most to gain before taking his thoughts to his father, the lord, so that a just and wise decision could be made. Yet, when hunting, he was a completely different man. He used wile and cunning to find the stag and let nothing stand in his way. The end for the stag was quick, violent and bloody, but then the devout young man would instantly kneel on the ground to thank his Lord Jesus Christ, expecting all of his entourage to do the same. Whether they had wonderful new clothes in the new fashion or not, they had to join him in prayer.

One day the young lord was deep in the forest with just one servant to look after his needs. When he saw movement between the branches he signalled to his servant to wait. He moved deeper and deeper into the forest, using his best hunting skills to move slowly towards his prey. His feet landed on the undergrowth as softly as a chiffchaff landing on a branch. He carefully transferred his weight from one foot to another when he was sure that no branches or twigs cracking would announce his approach.

His bow and arrow were poised as he carefully moved aside a curtain of leaves and fronds to reveal a fair lady, bathing in a small pool and clutching a gold necklace.

William involuntarily stepped back, all thoughts of stealth forgotten in his surprise at the sight before him. Leaves rustled around him and the maiden, suddenly alerted to his presence, immediately sought to cover her nakedness with her long blonde, almost silver, hair. Feeling sure that the woman, who had been clutching a gold necklace after all, was of high rank, the young lord stepped forward and awkwardly bowed to her. Incredibly she did not scold him or shout at him. Despite finding her in such a state of undress, she still appeared positively regal and, wishing to honour her as he would in a jousting competition, he offered her his handkerchief.

They started a slow and stilted conversation and it was as if she had never spoken English before. However, the conversation soon gathered pace. She introduced herself as Elioxe and was full of stories of life in other countries. The young lord, enchanted by these tales of far-off lands, asked how she could know about all of these places. The woman merely laughed, however, and said that she had crossed many oceans. This seemed impossible, how could she have visited such places and still look so youthful and beautiful? Her lips were deep ruby red and her neck was long and elegant. They talked through the night, sharing more than one or two kisses, and by the morning he had sworn that he would never be separated from her and that he would marry her.

They emerged from the forest with the young lady dressed in a long shirt belonging to the young lord and William himself bare-chested despite the cold. She still clutched the golden chain. Sending his servant ahead to the castle, the woman laid a graceful hand on William's arm and his eyes met hers for a moment as she said, in a quiet voice full of prophesy, 'I will bear you seven children and one of those children will forever bear the burden for our union'.

The young lord stared after her, perplexed, as they were ushered into the castle and borne away to the men's and the women's quarters. He tried to take up his usual routine the next morning by practising his skills with the bow and arrow. However, his thoughts constantly drifted back to Elioxe and he barely heard his friends bragging and joking around him. What would she make of his life here? Would she think that it was empty? Full of hunting prowess but not much more? He decided that he would not go back on his promise to marry Elioxe, despite the disappointment that this would bring his mother in particular.

So when the couple were summoned to talk to the Lord and Lady of the castle, William not only insisted that they would marry but pressed for a wedding as soon as possible. Elioxe, meanwhile, was more restrained and used the time to gain the measure of the Lord and Lady. The Lord of the castle, Ralph, was harmless and took his advice from his son and his wife. The Lady, Matrosilie, appeared soft on the surface, yet Elioxe sensed something harder and more menacing beneath her gentle exterior. Every comment, every smile, seemed innocent and friendly but Elioxe was not fooled. She was sure that Matrosilie had guessed her secret and know the meaning of the gold necklace that she clutched wherever she went. There was a streak of iron running through the Lady Matrosilie's character and Elioxe had much to fear.

The wedding took place surprisingly quickly. The ceremony had all of the solemnity expected for a member of the nobility. The wedding feast took place in rooms decorated opulently with finely woven tapestries, complemented with the sumptuous silks worn by the guests. Yet Elioxe outshone all of this. Her silver-blonde hair caught the light and the smiles on the face of bride and groom showed that they were truly happy.

It was no surprise when Elioxe revealed that she was pregnant soon after the wedding, yet the rate at which her stomach grew was astonishing. Some started to suspect that the couple had not waited until the marriage before consummating their union, and soon it became obvious that she was carrying more than one child. William's mother now began to sow the seeds of dissent. On the surface she appeared to be a mother-in-law doing everything she could to support her daughter-in-law. Yet scarcely a day went by when she did not make allusions to women meddling with witchcraft who gave birth to all manner of creatures.

As the day of Elioxe's confinement drew nearer, she had a feeling of foreboding. William dismissed her concerns, but when she went into labour, Elioxe found that Matrosilie intended to be her one and only attendant. A servant was on hand to bring towels and water when summoned, but Matrosilie would be the first to welcome each child into the world. Elioxe was uneasy but felt powerless to alter the arrangements. Soon she was hit by such an intense labour that she could not think any further than living through each wave of pain. Each child was born healthy and strong – six boys and one girl.

However, the babes were slightly different to normal human children – each was born with a golden chain around their neck. Elioxe knew at once that they shared a power that she had kept hidden from her husband. For the power of the golden chain meant that she could take the form of both swan and human. She was not ashamed of this. In the past her kind had helped form the lineage of many great kings. Kings who had brought peace and harmony to their people. But she knew that humans often feared such magic and had therefore kept this knowledge to herself.

When Elioxe woke, she found that she had been moved to a spartan room. There were no tapestries, nor the limewashed walls with paintings that the couple had enjoyed in their apartments. There were stone walls, a small cup of water and one small window overlooking the moat. Servants attended her but would not talk to her at all and even questions about her children could not prompt a reply. Elioxe became increasingly uneasy as she wondered what the servants – who were usually so gracious – might have been told.

When she looked out of the window, she saw a labourer digging a hole. Every so often he stopped, mopped his brow and measured the height of the hole. The feeling of foreboding increased and Elioxe could not escape the thought that the ever-lengthening hole was somehow linked to her imprisonment.

Finally Matrosilie and William entered her room. They each acknowledged her curtly and then Matrosilie nodded to a nearby servant and a number of puppies ran into the room. When the puppies immediately sought out Elioxe and began to lick her clothing, William looked stunned and quite deflated. Alarmed, Elioxe realised that Matrosilie has rubbed the scent of the puppies' mother on to her clothing. William had evidently been told that she was a witch who had given birth to seven dogs and his mother had just confirmed this for him. Matrosilie had been the only one to see her real children and had taken them away from her.

'It's not what you think my love. I can take another form, but not that of a dog. I am here to bring peace and understanding.' Elioxe cried in desperation. As William shrank back in disgust, she saw that she had only made matters worse – William now believed that she was an abomination, that she was deceitful and was trying to hide her wickedness. Elioxe was gripped with terror as she wondered what her mother-in-law might have done with her children.

The next morning, quiet and subdued, Elioxe was led to the hole and she took this as confirmation that they intended to silence her by killing her. She watched numbly as the men continued to dig – bringing each new spadesful of earth up to the surface and heaping it to one side. As she was taken by the arms and ordered to climb into the hole, she asked for one last word with her husband. From the panic in his eyes, it was clear that he did not know what to expect. Elioxe urgently whispered that he must look for their children and that he would know that they were his because they would all be clutching golden chains. Yes, she said, with a voice that trembled with anxiety, she could take on another form, but only that of a swan and as a helper for those who wished to rule wisely.

William had started to think of his wife with something like revulsion but now he was frightened. If she was right then his children were alive and he could well lose all of them. The prophesy that Elioxe had made when they first met came back to him. She had said that she would bear seven children and that one of those children would bear the burden of their union. What could it mean? Hastily he readied his horse and rode into the forest. He searched until he came to the small pool where they first met. Hurrying into the clearing, he found a young servant bathing six babies.

The lad was timorous at first, saying that he was answerable to Matrosilie only. William urged him to speak, saying, 'You will find me a good master in the future, but you must overcome your apprehensions now.' At that the young man broke down and confessed that Matrosilie had ordered him to kill the children. When the moment came, however, he could not murder seven babies. Ashamed, he also blurted out that he had taken one of the gold chains that the children were born with to be melted down by the goldsmith. Matrosilie had promised that he could keep the gold chains and they would have made his family rich. However, when the chain had been taken from the baby boy, he had transformed inexplicably into a young swan and the terrified servant had been too afraid to remove any of the other chains.

William gathered the reins of his horse and leapt into the saddle. He raced back to the castle, spurring his horse on in the hope that Elioxe would still be alive by the time that he returned. As he clattered through the castle gates he called for the execution to halt and for his wife to be set free. The next hour brought great joy and also great sadness. There was joy as Elioxe was freed unharmed and William openly begged for her forgiveness. But sadness as William revealed that one of their children had been robbed of his gold chain and was locked in the form of a swan. He had taken to the water and appeared to be lost to them forever. Elioxe did not need to remind him of the prophesy now, it all made too much sense and William knew that the boy trapped in the form of a swan would be the child to bear the weight of their union.

In the months to come many things changed. William's father died of a weak heart soon after the children were found, although many suspected that this was because he could not live with the part he had played in Elioxe's persecution. Matrosilie, meanwhile, would never admit the wrong that she had inflicted on William and his family, and was banished from the kingdom. Elioxe forgave William and they became the Lord and Lady of the castle, respected by their people. The five boys and one girl grew up to become powerful and wise members of the nobility but Elioxe and William never forgot their seventh child.

At the same time rumours began to reach them of a knightly swan. This swan ruled the waters as the eagle rules the sky. They heard of a swan rescuer pulling a boat to freedom, lost souls who found salvation from drowning because of the intervention of this knight. The swan showed purity, courage and valour and it was the only creature that the eagle deigned to fight. In fact the influence of the swan knight was so great that chivalric orders were set up in his honour.

Elioxe grew into the role of middle-aged matron and mother of six. Mostly she was happy but there were times when concern for her son the swan knight became too great. It was not unusual for William to find her sobbing. In his arms, she reproached herself for bringing such calamity upon the family. William comforted her as well as he could, assuring her that whatever he had lost by loving her, none was by her design.

Thus we almost end our story, except for an archaeological find in 1965. On the site of Dunstable Friary, a small brooch in the shape of a swan was found and assumed to be a livery badge. Yet the story persisted for many generations in Bedfordshire of Matrosilie's final revenge. For, you see, Matrosilie had magical powers of her own.

Her inability to accept Elioxe came not from a fear or distaste for all things magical, but rather she believed an ability to change forms was clear evidence that her new daughter-in-law was consorting with the Devil. Storytellers told how Matrosilie refused to accept that swans – honourable and regal that they are – could have nothing to do with the Devil's designs. Although old and frail, she searched for the knight swan whose bravery had created many tales of his own. When she found him, she transformed the swan into another form. He became solid, his wings taking the form of opaque white enamel and his beak and chain becoming pure gold. Shrinking the frozen form of the swan, she wore his body like a trophy until she lay upon her deathbed and then the jewel was hidden.

The small badge became known as the Dunstable Swan Jewel and can be found at the British Museum in the room dedicated to Medieval Europe. You can see it as an exquisite work of art – requiring the finest materials and painstaking workmanship – or as a testament to two women, one of whom persecuted the other because she could not understand her outward form, the other who lived a life overcoming that.

11

A Witch in a Bottle

The idea germinated as the Dunstable headmaster gazed proprietorially over the landscape. In the classrooms above him could be heard the muffled sounds of schoolboys ragging one of the masters, while closer to hand were the subdued sounds of a maid clearing the fireplace. When she left, the tang of ashes lingered in the air. Meanwhile, the headmaster stood in the bay window surveying the land that had become his home, his hands held stiffly behind his back. Even with no one else in the room, he moved his lanky frame awkwardly, like a dancing marionette.

He sighed, overwhelmed by the lushness and the soft undulations of the countryside before him. It moved him and was a constant source of comfort to him. His eyes darted upwards as he saw a hawk circling above. He knew from his hunting days that the creatures were devoid of affection. Yet the headmaster liked to think that these birds shared his affinity for the landscape. As he watched the hawk, his thoughts turned to the churchyard of St Peter's Priory. As a picture of the churchyard sprang to his mind, he could feel the lurking anger. It was an abomination, an ungodly home for vixen's dens and screeching owls. As he continued to gaze out of the window, an idea began to take hold, and then to flourish.

A botanist might be fond of the churchyard as a haven for wildlife. The headmaster, however, saw it as an affront. The rector refused to spend any money on it, concentrating instead on the church buildings, and with no gardener prepared to venture near it, the alder grew vigorously until it completely obscured the gravestones, the nettles chocked the pathways and the insects industriously shuffled leaf cuttings across the path.

Now the headmaster's formless idea became an inspiration. He moved with a grace that he did not know he possessed, sitting down and sweeping his fountain pen from his desk. He dipped his pen in the ink. As one bulbous drop gathered on the pen-tip, ready to plummet back into the inkpot, he permitted himself a moment of smugness. The modern fashion for Gothic tales might just help his cause.

The ink flowed across the page and the headmaster started to weave a tale. The first character to step out from the mist was Sally.

Sally ostensibly lived apart from the rest of her village. In a feudal society, people such as Sally lived a precarious life. She did not attend Mass, she did not gossip and she failed to flatter those who were most used to it. Thus the monks in the priory and the feudal lords frowned upon visits to her cottage, and Sally was aware that visitors to her cottage would skulk in the shadows before knocking at her door – hoping that nobody would notice them and ask any questions.

When they couldn't find Sally in her cottage, the visitors would huddle somewhere out of the way in order to wait for her. Sally would soon emerge from the forest, brushing aside branches with green stripes down her face. The stripes resulted from her habit of rummaging through mosses and then running her hands down her face as she pondered which poultice she would prepare with her finds. She felt part of nature in all its rawness. She could accept not just the warmth of a crisp spring day but also the fact that many of the small creatures in the forest would not survive a long hard cold winter.

Sally's acceptance and appreciation for the natural world gave her a sense of serenity that few of the monks understood. Nevertheless, it was not unknown for some of the senior monks to seek her out for advice, although this was usually after dark when they could be free from prying eyes. Sally usually listened intently. When the senior monk came to the crux of his story, there would be a long moment of silence. Then she would ask probing questions, give a suggestion that altered the perspective of the story and wait. Slowly, realisation would dawn and the monk would leave the cottage feeling much wiser, and unaware of Sally's role in gently guiding him towards that wisdom.

Maybe it was because of her skill with people that she saw the good and the bad in everyone and always sought to encourage the good. However, Sally's undoing was the fear and dark emotions that are part of bereavement. One evening Sally was sitting by the door of the cottage in the dusk light when she realised that a figure was standing by the edge of the forest. She beckoned him over. At first he did not move, and she could see his silhouette wavering with indecision. When he came forward, she realised that he was one of the merchant classes. Not one of those who toiled in the fields all day, but also not someone who prided himself on not having to work. He told her that his daughter was ill. It was obvious that he felt uncomfortable about visiting her and Sally tried to be soothing. Just at the moment when she was gaining his trust, a large black cat strolled onto the scene and with the air of one returning home after a long day, sat down next to Sally. The merchant eyed the cat with suspicion and Sally explained that she had never seen it before. It must be hoping for a meal, she said.

The merchant had regained his composure when Sally was distracted by finding a spray of silver cinquefoil on the ground. There had always been a mercurial unpredictability about Sally and those that knew her better would not have found this odd. There were moments when a villager would ask the most prosaic question to find that she became lost in her thoughts. Although they were Christians, they also believed in the old ways. They waited while she left her body, and followed the trails left by spirits. She would return to her body, look at them blankly and ask them to repeat their question. This merchant found himself unnerved by the combination of Sally's lost look and the black cat's apparent familiarity with her. He went to leave, hesitated momentarily and stumbled back to snatch the herbs that Sally grasped in her hand.

When he returned to his daughter's sick bed, he was unaware that his wife had noticed a difference in their daughter and the priest had already administered last rites. The merchant's mind was addled by hope and his mind raced, searching for a solution. As he wetted his daughter's lips with Sally's potion and urged her to take the odd sip, his wife prepared herself for what lay ahead. She eased her husband out of the room and turned her mind away from memories of her child before her illness. The last rites had given her little comfort. She could offer the love of a mother, holding her child's hand and catching the moment to softly sigh 'Let go, my love'. She knew when that moment was upon the girl as the rasping breaths became shallower and shallower. By the morning the merchant's daughter was dead and the merchant's thoughts grappled with the incomprehension of her passing.

His mind turned again and again to Sally. In his sorrow he gradually convinced himself that she was a witch and that she and her familiar – the black cat – had communed in the spirit world together. He saw clearly now that he had unwittingly brought into his household the potion that had murdered his poor sweet innocent daughter. His grief turned black and hard, and full of hatred for Sally. His poor wife worried that he would destroy those around him and poison his own soul. He told everyone that he met that Sally was a witch who had killed his daughter. The gossip spread but it lacked the vicious quality necessary for a witch-hunt. Many made the observation that the merchant was obviously heartbroken.

Sally, meanwhile, unwittingly made herself look guilty by taking in the black cat that had first adopted her when the merchant visited her. It was the unfortunate combination of her kindness with an abandoned cat and the merchant's wealth that made her arrest inevitable. All that was needed was a direct accusation and this was to come in the shape of a child starved of any attention, who found himself the centre of village life. The child described how he had seen Sally change into a black cat herself and how she and her familiar would prowl amongst the tombstones of the churchyard. This story silenced those who had sought to protect her. Before long, Sally was taken from her cottage and – with a look mingling fear and pride – she was marched through the village to be locked in a cellar at the priory.

A week later the ecclesiastical court was assembled. The peasants were given leave from the fields to watch Sally's arrival. Some looked shamefaced but others relished the opportunity to berate and humiliate her. When Sally passed them, shackled in a cart, she was stunned by the behaviour of the villagers. Men who had accepted words of kindness and a poultice now spat and swore at her. Weak and dishevelled, Sally was hauled in front of the court. Passively she listened to the witnesses who swore on the Bible and then told fantastical and fabricated stories of her life as a witch. When she was asked if she had anything to say for herself, she merely shrugged, and when they read out the sentence that she would be burnt to death, she gawped at the bishop convening the court.

Her behaviour was taken as an admission of truth. In fact it was part of her dawning realisation that, as an outsider, she was dispensable and easily betrayed. The time of the burning was set at noon the following day and Sally's fear quickly became unbearable and overwhelming. A priest visited her cell and asked if she would like to make her last confession but Sally merely sneered a reply and turned her back on him, refusing to speak. He left and as the door closed behind him, the guards heard a brief inconsolable cry.

As Sally came to terms with her approaching death, the villagers also anticipated the event. Peasants flocked from neighbouring villages for the entertainment and in the anonymity of increased numbers, men and women allowed themselves to feel excitement and for that excitement to gather.

When she was brought out to the stake, the crowd were baying for her blood. Cowed by the noise, she was silent as she was tied to the stake. As a man moved forward with a flaming torch and set the small branches alight, she let out a scream. The flames licked closer and closer to Sally and the crowd jostled one another to gain the first sight of her beginning to burn. As the smell of burning flesh drifted towards the crowd, the more sensitive retched and even those who had been excited winced momentarily. Plumes of smoke billowed into the crowd, creating a white smoky curtain that obscured everything but the face of the person next to them. It was as this curtain descended that a scream and a curse rent the air. The power of that curse hit everyone in the crowd like a body blow, pulsing through the mass of people in the direction of the priory. The smoke lifted, leaving a shambling, fearful mass of people.

The crowd dispersed quickly. Sally's bones were taken and buried in unconsecrated land, and the town tried to carry on as if nothing had happened. That was not to be. They knew that with a curse that strong they would feel the consequences before long. No one dared to say the words of the incantation. It had held such sinister power and it was much too dangerous to repeat. The change came with a whisper, soft sounds in the peasants' cottages that could not be explained. Soon villagers were attuned to the slightest noise at night and they were not surprised when the soft sounds became rapping on the walls and unexplained footsteps.

At the priory all of the pet animals deserted the building and grounds. Monks noticed that extinguished candles mysteriously relit. During the Mass, monks saw shadowy figures from the corner of their eyes. In the library, the monks found books tumbled in a heap on the floor, knowing that they had been stacked in an orderly fashion by a junior brother. The prior found his keys had been moved and his books moved around his desk. They all had Sally's curse ringing in their ears and the prior's conscience was stung. He was aware that Sally had always been a wise woman of herbs, like her mother before her. It had been the depth of their betrayal that had moved Sally to curse the priory using some arcane knowledge that her mother had passed on to her.

Reluctantly the prior called a 'palmer', a man who had learnt the art of luring spirits. He arrived from Bristol on a Sunday morning, attended Mass and was a subtle and quiet presence around the priory for the next three days. Eventually he asked the prior to meet him at midnight in the priory, bringing with him eleven monks of his choosing. They spent hours praying – preparing themselves for calling Sally's spirit. When the palmer called on Sally's spirit, the temperature began to drop. The monks exchanged fearful looks, concerned that it was their own imagination overcoming them, but even more afraid that it was a signal of Sally's presence.

Moments passed. The candle flames flicked as if a disembodied spirit had walked past. Then one of the monks began to talk in a childlike voice that was not his own, his face becoming contorted as he tried to regain control over his body. The palmer raised his voice, calling on Sally to leave the holy place of the priory. In response he was hit with a mighty force around the head and thrown to the ground. The dazed palmer struggled upright and pulled out a dusky green mottled bottle from within his cloak. Shaped like a bloated pig's-bladder, it looked harmless. He pulled out the cork and placed the bottle on the altar, signalling to the monks to move away from the altar. The palmer had heard Sally's story and realised that her spirit would not rest easily.

In the past three days he had searched the forlorn cottage where Sally had lived, looking for anything that had belonged to her, anything that would remind her of her corporeal life and lure her to him. He had stooped as he stepped into her lowly hovel, her lack of possessions showing how little she had wanted for herself. Some of her potions rested in bowls in a corner and he swept them into a sack, then continued to hunt for something more personal to her. Eventually he found a scrap of clothing, some hair on her bedding and a dried flower that she had kept for herself. Before he left he dug up a small handful of soil; this would hold the memories and the aromas of her life.

Taking over a small corner of the priory kitchen, the palmer had asked for a bottle and stopper to be brought to him. The clothing was unravelled and small threads placed at the bottom of the glass bottle, he took a phial containing an unknown liquid and added two or three drops before adding the soil, Sally's hairs and one of the potions that she had left in her cottage.

Now the palmer was in the priory, the cork removed from the bottle and the spirit of Sally was acutely aware of smells that made her long for the life she had had before – a life in which she had felt fulfilled. The attraction of the bottle was irresistible for Sally. As she moved closer to the bottle, the monks formed a circle around it, each of them grasping a crucifix. Sally was now trapped and she squirmed into the bottle, hoping that this was a place of safety. Soon she was to realise her mistake. As soon as she slipped down the glass neck, the palmer darted over with the cork closing up the bottle for ever.

Sally's wailings were heard by some of the monks in the dormitories as the bottle was rushed outside into the graveyard. The palmer had not only been busy creating a lure for Sally but had also organised a safe place for the bottle. An old workman stood leaning on his shovel in front of a large hole waiting for the palmer's approach. Once the glass bottle was lowered gently into the hole, the workman covered it with soil, oblivious to the driving rain. The palmer let out a sigh of relief when the workman patted down the soil to show that he had finished. Only once the bottle had been buried did the palmer allow the monks into the graveyard – he was determined that the location of the bottle would remain secret.

In the days that followed, the monks waited to see if the haunting would continue. At first it seemed eerily quiet, as if this was the calm before the storm. However, as life remained peaceful, the monks in the priory realised that they no longer needed to constantly look over their shoulders. Nevertheless, aware that Sally's spirit had been captured and buried in the graveyard, none of them could be persuaded to tend the graves. From that point on the monks would not cut back a tree that had forced its way on to a path lest Sally's bottle had leaked and was tending to its needs. Nor would they weed or pick flowers for the graves.

And this is the story that the headmaster wrote one winter's evening in his study, he even wrote a poem to accompany it. With the fashion for Gothic novels, his writing was the talk of the gentlemen and gentlewomen in the county. It was, of course, no coincidence that this revealed the scandalously unkempt state of the local priory churchyard. The poem was catchy and local lads memorised it, quoting it to the rector there. The rector was furious. Within months he had organised a two-day bazaar, which raised one thousand pounds towards the restoration of the churchyard. And so the wily headmaster had his way and the churchyard was restored.

We finish with some words from the poem, demonstrating that the pen is mightier than the sword, especially when faced with an unruly churchyard.

> The spirit in the bottle
> Go softly where you treade
> The lady is a cunning one
> Disturb ye not the wicked dead
>
> Never tarry on a restless night
> Lest ye find what darkness means
> For she will trouble thee till in sleep
> And steal thy soul through dream

12

SIR ROWLAND ALSTON'S SOUL

Sir Rowland Alston was the epitome of suave. Whatever he wanted seemed to fly to his fingertips. As a member of the aristocracy, his place within society was assured. Yet opinion was divided on how exactly he had secured his inexorable rise to power. For the local villagers of Odell, however, there was no debate – they knew that Sir Rowland had sold his soul. They saw the reality of his character, stripped of the fake charm that he showed to those of his own class.

He was not merely neglectful, as that was almost to be expected. Few landowners troubled themselves with the fate of their tenants. He was not merely a wastrel, as that would have raised few eyebrows. Landowners were renowned for squandering their income. Maybe they would landscape their estates, or build a folly. And if that failed to bankrupt them then there was always gambling or drinking. No, Sir Rowland was both of these things and more.

Some said that what was marked about Sir Rowland was the malice he showed towards his tenants. If there was even the merest intimation of criticism, the perpetrator would find themselves arrested for theft or poaching. He would make sure that they never saw their loved ones before they were hanged or transported. He seemed to enjoy the bewildered and distraught looks on the faces of the condemned as they scanned a courtroom or crowd for their loved ones. Yet to those in power, his pliable face seemed to be that of a man who was honest and whose only possible fault was his very frankness.

Yet even such spitefulness was not unheard of. What made Sir Rowland different from his contemporaries was his sheer luck. If he fell, he never hurt himself. If he gambled, he never lost money. If he fought a duel, he always won. His harvests never failed and whatever he ate and drank, he was always healthy. It seemed he had the luck of the Devil.

The church of All Saints is just outside the village, with a steep slope running up to the entrance. The slope is punishing for late-comers, who find themselves just a tad more conspicuous than they hoped as they try to catch their breath and merge in with the rest of the congregation. Over the course of the early months of the year, parishioners comment on the bluebells pushing their way up through the stones. On an overcast day with the sun nudging its way through the clouds, it was a place to take your troubles and leave feeling more peaceful. Sir Rowland, however, did not feel like that about the church. He was not one for admiring the landscape or appreciating the flowers, and he could never seem to get to the church on time.

One night, there was a hammering on the door of Sir Rowland's country home. When the maid answered, she asked the man standing there for his hat and coat, all the time feeling a fierce urge to run. This instinct to be as far away from him as possible was overwhelming and there was no perceptible reason to explain it. His gaze seemed to sear its way into her very soul but later she could not give any description of him, not even to say what colour eyes he had.

With a sweep of his long black coat, he strode towards Sir Rowland's study. Obviously he needed no direction. The poor maid stared after him, her mouth partly open. She shook herself out of her stupor, convinced that she looked like an imbecile.

Then later, knowing she was expected to offer visitors food and drink, she knocked hesitantly on the door. 'Beggin' your pardon sir.' At this she found that her nerves had overcome her and she had swallowed her words. She fought to regain her composure. 'Will you be wantin' anything to eat or drink?' Looking timidly into the study, she realised that the usually suave Sir Rowland was now looking dishevelled and, with his head bowed, she heard him mumble, 'No, you may go.' She was shocked. Her master was always in control, yet now he looked a broken man. The stranger turned slowly towards her. 'Our business is almost finished. Thank you.'

The maid was upstairs, preparing the fire in her master's bedroom for the next morning when she heard scuffling downstairs followed by doors slamming. She ran to the top of the stairs, peering over them to see Sir Rowland hastily pushing servants to one side or into the path of the strange man, who followed close behind him. Sir Rowland bolted out of the door and leapt on to the jet-black horse of the stranger. He pulled back viciously on the reins and kicked the horse hard in its flanks. The stranger appeared and called for Sir Rowland's horse. Nobody contemplated denying him anything he asked for. He said nothing but he was a malevolent brooding presence as he waited the few minutes needed to wake the horse and ready it.

The stranger hurtled after Sir Rowland as soon as the bit was fitted into the horse's mouth. All of the servants were standing at the front of the manor house now, watching the riders' progress across the landscape. Despite riding another man's horse using another man's harness, Sir Rowland moved the black horse through the landscape without hesitation. Like water flowing down a hill, he moved gracefully and gathered pace. The stranger urged on Sir Rowland's horse and it sprinted faster than any of the household had ever seen it run, causing the distance between the two men and horses to narrow.

Sir Rowland plunged into woodland at the first opportunity. Used to hunting foxes, it was now his turn to be the prey. He took the horse over small streams, dodging overhanging branches. Still, behind him there were glimpses of movement and he knew that the sinister stranger was relentlessly following him. When he left the woodlands, the servants thought that he had thrown the man off his tracks. Then a minute later the stranger appeared.

The deadly pursuit continued, neither man seemed to be flagging and they were now headed uphill towards All Saints church. Surely Sir Rowland intended to seek sanctuary there. For a brief second the two men were in the same field, and Sir Rowland glanced round to check just before there was a black blur and the horse vaulted over the hedge. From their vantage point, the servants watched as the stranger gained on Sir Rowland inch by inch.

Sir Rowland reached the church with the stranger close behind him. The familiarity of the church, with the moss nestled between the upright stones of the church wall and the ivy coiled around the trees, assuaged his anxiety momentarily. He threw himself out of the saddle, pebbles and small stones crunched and ricocheted as he landed on the path. Squeezing himself through the door, he slammed it sharply on the stranger's fingertips as they grasped the doorframe. As he bolted the church door a faint sulphurous smell drifted across the threshold. A voice rumbled, ordering him to come out and pay back his debt, but he simply cowered in a corner, hoping that the man, who was no stranger to him, would go away.

The next morning, the servants waited for Sir Rowland to return. Eventually the butler and a footman walked to the church to see if they could find him. They had heard noises from the church during the night, and so were nervous about what they would find. As they approached the porch of the church, the harsh grating sound of crows cawing resounded in their ears. When they reached the church door they were surprised to find themselves locked out and imprinted on the stone porch were five giant burn marks in the shape of fingerprints.

The local vicar was found and a small group of villagers clustered around the church, excited by the idea that something with a whiff of the Gothic was happening in their village. The vicar, avoiding eye contact with the bystanders, prised open a small window and a young boy wriggled through the space. After a few moments, the child reappeared, opening the large wooden church door. His eyes were wide with horror. Sir Rowland had crawled towards the font and his hand, which rested on its base, was twisted, reaching upwards.

The villagers could not prove it but, to them, it was obvious what had happened. Sir Rowland had made a deal with the Devil and the Devil had come to collect his debt. When Sir Rowland tried to escape, the Devil had chased him, hoping to intercept him before he reached the sanctuary of the church. Sir Rowland made it to safety just in time but – perhaps believing that his sins were too great to be protected, even by the consecrated grounds of a church – he literally scared himself to death.

Even in death Sir Rowland's servants feared their former master and, frightened that he might reach them from beyond the grave if they did not honour his body, they gave no opposition when the priest suggested a Christian burial.

For months the scandal of Sir Rowland's death meant that sightseers came to look at the scorch marks on the church porch. Eventually the flood of visitors became one or two well-read tourists visiting every so often. Rumours persist that Sir Rowland's ghost will return every hundred years riding a jet-black horse with the Devil riding a horse close behind him.

The manor house was burnt down in 1931 and stood as a testament to the fading power of the Alstons. Despite its slow disintegration, there was still a certain solemnity to the architecture. In fact many felt they could detect pride and scorn in the walls. The glass had been blasted from the windows and the walls were crumbling.

The house became a den for two small boys in the last year of the Second World War. One day they ran back home to tell their mothers about the black horse ridden by a man smartly dressed in a suit, followed quickly by another more menacing horseman. As the details of the story tumbled out the women realised that Sir Rowland had visited his ancestral home one more time before vanishing. Local legend prophesies that his next visit will be in 2044.

13

SAINT CYNEBURGA

There were very few holy wells recorded before the Domesday Book of William the Conqueror. Chalgrave has one of them. The site itself was called Kimberwell and was noted by chroniclers in 926 before the Norman invasion. Pilgrims visited the well for hundreds of years for the healing properties of the spring. This is the story of how the well gained its reputation for curing the sick.

Cyneburga looked on incredulously at the court of her father. She had never heard such a story before and was quite amazed that Penda the pagan king would allow a man to talk of the new God, the Christian God. Cyneburga took little notice of the rich hangings used to decorate the walls, nor of the smell of the honeyed meat cooking on the griddle nearby. Instead she stared at the Christian man with something close to disgust. How could her father let the man into the court, with his fantastical tales of just one God? And a God that would let his own son die painfully.

Penda was a huge man, built like a rock with a laugh that shook the timbers of the great hall. Later Penda would be described as a king who was motiveless and destructive, spreading wanton terror amongst his neighbours. Yet this was not the man that Cyneburga, his daughter, knew. Yes, he could be ruthless. As the ruler of

Mercia he had been penned in on all sides, the Northumbrians to the north of him, the Britons in the west, the East Angles in the east and the West Saxons to the south of them. Living with these kingdoms around him, he was used to waging war. But Penda was also a man of integrity, he expected his children to obey the god in whom they believed and allowed them to choose whether they would be pagan or Christian.

Some of the kings in other kingdoms were entertaining Christian ideas. Penda saw no problem with allowing such preachers into his court. Now Cyneburga was faced with a missionary Christian called Edward. Edward was a squat, grubby and flat-bottomed man, who was preaching and describing a man called Jesus who had allowed himself to be nailed to a cross and then raised from the dead. Edward was not a natural orator, and with his squat figure and lack of charisma he was the antithesis of Cyneburga's father. The court laughed derisively when the preacher described a man who was meek, forgiving and lived a life of simplicity. Cyneburga was usually calm, yet she found herself reacting to Edward's confidence with scorn. The hall was hushed as she said that she could not listen to him any more and asked him to leave.

Yet that night Cyneburga found herself thinking about what the preacher had said and she started to think of questions that she wanted to ask him. She remembered that she had lost patience with him when he was telling the story of the sower, calling it a parable. She now realised that she wanted to find out more and wished she had not spoken to him so scathingly. She sent out a messenger asking him to return to the court. When she received a reply that she must come to him, she set off on horseback through the driving rain to bring him back to the court.

The next few weeks turned her world upside down. She admitted doubts about the bleakness that was a part of her people's stories and poetry. She found something special within the Christian parables and the life of prayer that was offered. Once she brought this Christian God into her life, many things made sense to her. She was baptised within the month.

Penda was not overjoyed about this new development but he was accepting of all kinds of gods and he could see some advantages to this new development. Cyneburga needed to make a good match and now that she was a Christian, it could mean an advantageous alliance. Cyneburga's father was a colossus of the time, holding together a large kingdom. He was the pre-eminent warrior and skilled at diplomatic alliances. Moreover, he knew the reality of his situation – he was hemmed in on all sides by enemies and could not risk too many fights at once. Alliances could mean the difference between a 'friendly' neighbouring kingdom, which negotiated borders and trade, and a hostile one that might invade without warning or pretext. The problem was that Cyneburga had started to develop her own ideas about her religious calling, and marriage had not been part of God's plan for her.

So Penda approached his daughter to discuss possibilities. He listened patiently as she described the religious life that she had been called for, living in a religious community with nuns who prayed and lived a life of simplicity as Jesus had done. He listened patiently and then gently reminded her about her place in life. She had been born into a family that depended upon the orchestration of an advantageous marriage so joining such a community was not an option. Cyneburga prayed and Penda thought about how to give his daughter something of what she had yearned for. Eventually it was announced that she would marry Alhfrith, son of Oswiu, King of Northumbria.

Christianity was flourishing in Northumbria after a previous ruler had brought in missionaries. The King of Northumbria was a vassal king to Penda and Penda knew much of the intrigues at his court. He knew that Cyneburga would find a comfortable place there and, for reasons of his own, Alhfrith would agree to a chaste marriage.

Cyneburga travelled to the Northumbrian court nervous of her reception. Her father had briefly ruled here in his own right, bringing back worship of the pagan gods for a time. How would they feel about her? She looked over the countryside. This was an alien world to her; very different from what she had known a few days' journey back. She thought fondly of the countryside where she was born. She had enjoyed growing up with the rolling hills and rivers.

She glanced again at the new landscape. A rocky outcrop cast ribbons of shadow over the fields. Trees grew twisted against the winds. It would be difficult to grow crops here and the lure of the gods of the trees, wind and thunder must be strong. She knew that she must have no other god now and to reveal the truth of Christ to others. At her journey's end, servants bustled around, moving her bags and readying her rooms. A woman, her dark hair threaded through with grey, moved powerfully through the crowd. Servants looked up at her approach and deferentially moved to one side. The woman grasped Cyneburga's hands and they looked upon each other face to face. Cyneburga had finally met Eanfled, her new mother-in-law, who would come to be a great influence on her life.

Cyneburga was married with little ceremony the next morning. Her first sight of Alhfrith was just before the ceremony, and not promising. He barely gave her a glance and as soon as the marriage was declared, he left her to change his clothing. During the feast following the marriage she sat with Alhfrith on one side and Eanfled on her other. Eanfled wanted to know more about her life growing up in a pagan court and her conversion, and Cyneburga replied haltingly. She knew little of the manuscripts that Eanfled mentioned or the Roman ways that Eanfled talked about but she liked and respected her mother-in-law from that point on.

Alhfrith and Cyneburga formed an uneasy chaste friendship in the coming months but it was with Eanfled that the strongest bond was formed. The two women shared a fierce intelligence and a strong faith. They prayed together and discussed the greatest religious issue of the time, which was the difference in practices between the Celtic Christian church and the Roman Christian church. She heard that her sister and all of her brothers had converted to Christianity, the tide was moving in their favour and away from her father Penda.

Encouraged by Eanfled, Cyneburga begged Alhfrith to end their marriage, which had never been consummated, allowing her to dedicate herself to the religious life. Her sister Cyneswitha, now also a Christian, had always admired Cyneburga's determination and joined her in founding Castor convent. The two now had something to use their boundless energy for. They learnt quickly, setting up records of tenants, rents and alms, and it gave both of them the chance to visit their birthplace with its uplands and downlands. Cyneburga enjoyed her vocation managing the Church's lands and teaching. However, her father was often in her thoughts and her prayers. As the power of Alhfrith's father Oswiu waxed like the moon, growing larger and brighter every day, so did the power of Penda wane.

Penda drew together forces from many kingdoms, intending to reassert his overlordship. Cyneburga never did find out how her father lost the battle and indeed his life. With such a loose alliance of warriors from other kingdoms, she suspected that some changed allegiance at the last moment, perhaps enticed by the promise of land or eternal life with a Christian king. She knew her father's thoughts on the subject of the afterlife. He had said that he would rather burn

in hell with his brave pagan ancestors, than spend an eternity in the Christian heaven. Her father was someone she would have to mourn privately.

Cyneburga's influence continued to grow. She corresponded with her erstwhile family, including her brother Paeda who had married into the Northumbrian royal family. She learnt of a growing divide between King Oswiu and her ex-husband Alhfrith; Oswiu practiced Celtic Christian practices and Alhfrith took a pragmatic view of the power of the Roman Church. Cyneburga was in the background at the Synod of Whitby bringing peace and reconciliation. The Synod decided that the Church would follow Roman traditions and was of huge significance, the after-effects would be felt down the centuries.

On her deathbed, Cyneburga's last thoughts were of the gulf that existed between herself and her father. She prepared herself to meet her maker, knowing that her father as a pagan would be in hell and forever lost to her. When she died her bones were kept at the convent and pilgrims visited the convent to pray and venerate them. What started as a trickle of pilgrims became a steady flow. She was made a saint and, after the Viking invasions, her bones were moved to Peterborough Abbey. The bones became an important relic for the abbey and thus an important source of income. She was much revered in Bedfordshire. Followers flocked to a well at Chalgrave believing she was born in the village and had returned often, blessing the well. Although it is not apparent on the landscape today, St Cyneburga's well in Chalgrave was considered a holy and blessed place.

14

LACE

Irene lived and breathed to sew and lace. At the age of seven she had started at lace school. Pale-faced from troubles at home, she expected to have her nose rubbed in pins for making a mistake. To her own surprise, as well as that of the teachers, she proved to be a quick learner. Her hands moved the bobbins as quickly as moving water, pausing momentarily before creating the next stitch. She loved the 'tells', the songs, for they were the music to her own intricate dances of shape and colour that she created on the fabric. Her favourite as a child was 'Needlepin, Needlepin' as it had a regular and jolly rhythm. She lost herself in the chanting and created lace-stitches that were exactly the same size. With that tell as her background, she anticipated moving the bobbins as the tell told her to 'work the lady out of the ditch'. Irene grew up saying little but quietly confident and ready to help others.

When she left the lace school at fourteen, she was invited to work with a family of lace workers called the Miltons, all of them experienced. She was told to sit next to the twins, Jane and Molly Milton, who were close in age to her. They showed her the candle-blocks that were positioned above their workplaces. These were wooden blocks holding a candle at the centre and four glass spheres that were filled with water and reflected the light in its purest form. In this pure white light and peaceful silence, Irene enjoyed her work. They could not sit anywhere near the fire in case a spark set the lace on fire so instead they placed earthenware pots filled with ashes close to their feet to warm them. The companionable silence was broken by the twins calling each other skinny, scatty and little pickle. Slowly, they pulled her into their easy friendship.

The silence was also broken by tells when the pace of work was flagging, only now the tells were darker, not at all coy, but describing the complicated domestic lives of lace workers in Bedfordshire at the time. Her favourite tell now had a waltz rhythm, the same melody repeated over and over. She smiled with Jane and Molly at the line, 'Father whipped mother and mother whipped me' and they forced themselves to keep a steady line when the tell described the father cutting himself up into wee little bits. How on earth was he meant to cut himself up into bits, let alone wonder at his own naughty tricks? The tells were bizarre and earthy, irreverent and entertaining.

Her sharp eyesight, her sense of touch and her whole being was channelled into the intricate patterns she made lacing. She had such skill that when shown a foreign piece of lace, she could identify the stitches used and prick out the pattern on to an animal hide. Such was her concentration that when a fine young man was shown around she barely noticed him. Nicholas Pudephat, who was considering buying a fine set of gentleman's handkerchiefs, was tall and handsome with fine features.

Later, he contrived to meet Irene and told her that he was impressed by her artistic talent and by her commitment to her work. He did not say that when he marvelled at her skill, he also revelled in the new image she could create of him. She did not know that he had fallen in love with the vision of a picture of himself on a lace handkerchief, with a fine woven pattern just coyly revealing itself above the edge of his pocket or a lace ruff so like pictures he had seen of the king. Irene was swept along by the flattery and Nicholas' good looks. When they married she did not mind how little work Nicholas did, he was studying and she was skilled enough to work from home on her own and choose who she would work for.

Nicholas found Irene plainer than he would have liked but she was unlikely to question him about his prospects and to disagree with his opinions, so he found himself generally happy. Many had been warned by their mothers to start as you mean to go on with a young gentleman and not to take any nonsense but Irene had had precious little time with her own mother and no one to guide her on the rocky road to adulthood. So she earned all of the money and did all of the domestic work as well. Nevertheless, during their evening together, Nicholas would often admire her work, and then an early night with the lights off meant she was happy. When she started to develop a cough, Nicholas did not notice. Irene asked Molly and Jane to help her when her condition steadily worsened – she did not want Nicholas to become unhappy with her and that seemed inevitable to her if she kept a poor house.

One evening Nicholas found Irene in bed, white, gaunt and her breath rattling. He ran, stumbling in his haste, to the Miltons' cottage. Molly heard somebody rapping the knocker repeatedly. On opening the door, she found Nicholas looking wan and haggard, and quickly followed him to the small cottage that he shared with Irene. Molly told him earnestly how much she loved Irene and that her family would do everything that was needed. She slipped out and minutes later, quietly and unobtrusively, Molly and her family took over Irene's care. The smell of herbs permeated the air in the kitchen, overwhelming and insinuating itself into every corner. Nicholas heard the tells from Irene's youth being sung, 'lead the lady out of the ditch', and from the harmonious times with the Miltons, 'She's earned a penny, she's spent a groat, she's burnt a hole in her holiday coat'. The family would chat to her about happenings in the village and then sing more. 'My shoes are to borrow, my husband to seek. For I cannot get married till after next week.'

Nicholas had some instinct that it was near the end-time when the hustle and bustle began to slow, Irene's breathing was hardly audible and a hush settled. When Irene asked to speak to him, he leaned over her carefully as if she would break. Every breath was stale and musty. He managed to hide his distaste and so did not react to what she said. It was only after the quiet breathing died down to nothing that Molly took her pulse and then slowly let her hand go and nodded to him, that he realised that her dying request was to be buried with her finest lace work and he had not had a chance to persuade her out of the idea.

After she was buried, the vision of the lace work in the coffin with her kept coming back to him. Surely she did not mean that? Surely the lace ruff using the latest French designs would look very fine on him and she would have wanted him to wear it? Nicholas became obsessed with the idea of recovering the lace work, telling villagers that he had buried his finest poetry with her and now no longer had the words to describe the love that he had for her. To everyone he seemed to be pining for his lost love but they recoiled when he even hinted at recovering his poetry.

Months later the spark was provided by a travelling Gypsy, who told him, 'if you dig hard enough you will discover the secret to your past and decide your future'. He waited till the evening when he gathered a spade, a lantern and a roll of linen to wrap the lace in when he found it. He told himself that he just wanted one last look at the lace work. He began digging with incredible energy, fuelled by the fear of being found. He found a couple of small bones but carried on digging regardless. The spade hit the coffin with a dull thud and he jumped into the hole to clear away the remaining soil. Raising the lid, his eyes surveyed the inside of the coffin with growing horror until he saw a small package tucked behind the dry remains of Irene's hand. His hand reached out as he imagined how fine he would look in the ruff. His hand came closer and his fingernails had just scraped Irene's thumb-bone when he heard her sweet voice singing, 'Father whipped Mother and Mother whipped me'.

Looking up, Nicholas saw Irene's ghost looming above him. She smiled at him, her lips scarlet red and her eyes luminously reproachful. Pretending not to be afraid, he spoke to the ghost, and said: 'What hast thou done with thy cheeks so red?'

'All withered and wasted away,' replied the ghost, in a hollow tone.

'What hast thou done with thy soft hair?'

'All withered and wasted away.'

'What hast thou done with thy lace?'

'THOU HAST IT!'

Nicholas was scarcely able to breathe as he asked, 'What dost thou want with me?'

The ghost floated towards him and the lace was draped over his broad shoulders. 'Oh Nicholas,' she said, caressing the spot on the back of his neck that she knew made him go weak, 'you know what I want.' And as she said it she simultaneously pulled at the strings of the ruff, choking him as she cried, 'YOU, MY DARLING'.

Some say that even in death there was a small part of Irene that was forever gentle and that this gentleness in her soul meant that she could not end his life. He escaped with a long red line around his neck like the brand of a hangman's noose and drifted desultorily from job to job and tavern to tavern with a long scarf

of red silk tied raffishly round his neck. Others say that his body was found by the Miltons, who, attuned to the thoughts of Irene in death as well as life, simply tipped his body into the ground and used the spade to heap the soil back on to his body. When churchgoers arrived the next morning the sun shone brightly over the calm and peaceful churchyard. As for what really happened, we will never know.

Thank you to Aragon Lace Makers who helped me to research this story. The lace makers move their bobbins around the cushion at great speed. The very experienced lace makers can move their bobbins at such a pace that it becomes a blur. Not only are they an extremely friendly group of people with a good taste in biscuits, but they are also quiet and unassuming experts. You can find them on Facebook.

15

THE DEVIL'S FAVOURITE GAME

In the years after the English Civil War, we were a serious nation. The maypole had been removed from village greens, including that of Marston Moretaine, and games, excessive drinking and theatre-going had been banned by those who espoused Puritan views. Holy Scripture was studied and widely preached by the godly, who sought to purify both the people of Britain and the Church as well.

The village church of St Mary was unusual as its tower was separate from the church building. Legend said that when the church was being built, the Devil tried to steal the tower away. When god-fearing folk stood in his way, he pushed the tower and church building apart so that he could sit at the top of the tower encouraging wrongdoing.

The local vicar sometimes wondered if the Devil was still at the top of the tower. He believed that dancing round the maypole corrupted not only those who danced but those who watched it as well. He knew that his flock was mostly a lost cause and needed constant reminding of their wrongdoings. Going to church on Sunday was a cheerless affair. The local vicar railed against his flock for their sinful thoughts.

If Josiah thought that the excited clergyman looked like a goose raising and flapping its wings as he called on God the Almighty, then he would certainly have kept his thought to himself. Were his cheeky son, Jed, to say the same, then he would be certain to receive a clip round the ear. As the villagers trooped out of the church doing their best to look sombre, the children would sidle away as soon as their parents began to chat. If any young boy or girl thought that the trees looked inviting and the branches were enticing them over, then they would certainly have resisted the temptation to start climbing.

One Sunday, Jed sat patiently all the way through the sermon. He did not whisper to his neighbour, he left the church respectfully and stayed with his parents rather than sneaking off to climb trees as he really wanted to. It was when he saw an inflated pig's bladder left abandoned by the edge of the woods that the trouble began. It had obviously been used as part of a game and now it lay gleaming in the sun and it seemed to be skulking there, waiting for him to pick it up.

At first he moved the bladder around like a ball as he ran around the fields on his own, but very soon other children joined him. They passed it to one another and intercepted it as the mood changed. At a particularly good tackle, the children roared out in appreciation and the adults turned en masse to stare at them, before returning to their conversations. As players became tired, other children took their place. The play ebbed and flowed up and down the field, and so did the excitement. To the children it was a complicated dance with players weaving in and out of play, but the adults were alarmed now. This looked raucous and unseemly for a Sunday.

Some of the adults came over to take the ball away from the children but they couldn't resist the temptation to just dribble with the ball for a few moments. Of course, within minutes all of the adults were swept into the game and the field resounded with laughter. The vicar, meanwhile, had been talking to a couple inside the church. Hearing the noise from outside, his face changed colour until it perfectly matched the white-washed church around him and his back was now as straight as the maypole he so despised. He stopped talking. This was quite a relief to the young man and his wife, who were terrified of the austere vicar. Stupefied, he swayed on the spot and then marched out of the church looking thunderous.

The sight that greeted him was of all the churchgoers enjoying themselves. Those who were not playing football were on the sidelines cheering enthusiastically. One of the young men had rushed home for his fiddle. As he started to play a couple of the women were dancing, albeit guardedly, hoping not to catch anyone's attention. The vicar shouted at the villagers and everything stopped. Then after a moment's reflection, the noise started to swell again. The vicar bellowed warnings but they had obviously decided that they worked hard during the week and went to church on Sundays. Now was the time to enjoy themselves.

In the following weeks, the villagers of Marston Moretaine seemed to lose patience with trying to keep to the Church's view of what was right. They were going to be condemned by their vicar whatever they did so why not enjoy a drink on Sunday and a game of cards? The vicar spoke to the bishop but nobody was able to remonstrate with the inhabitants of Marston Moretaine. As far as they were concerned, they had rediscovered their sense of fun and they were not about to go back to the grim existence that they had had before. Warnings of the Devil were ignored. They still went to church but the vicar, ranting in the pulpit, pointing out the worst culprits and spouting eternal damnation, became such a common event that they scarcely noticed it any more.

That was until the vicar, without even noticing it, found a threat that they would take seriously. 'And you unworthy sinners,' resonated throughout the church, 'this has come to the attention of Oliver Cromwell himself. He is a holy man and would come here himself to save your souls.' Jed's father, Josiah, heard much of the rest of the sermon, but he did not comprehend what was being said.

The vicar stood in front of him, but he might as well have ben mouthing the words. In Josiah's ears, his heart was louder than a blacksmith's hammer hitting the anvil as he thought of all that a visit from Cromwell could mean for the villagers. And then, out of his fear, an idea – drastic but necessary – was forged.

With the threat of a visit from Cromwell, over the next few weeks Josiah seemed to change personality completely. He took on a completely respectable facade, engaging the vicar in conversation about scripture and showing an earnestness that the villagers had never seen before. A couple of his friends challenged him and were dubious about this new approach to life. Especially when at the end of a diatribe quoting their local vicar at length, he then winked at them and walked away. Later they would visit him at home and ask what exactly he was planning.

One Sunday, the village was following its usual pursuits. Playing football, playing the violin and dancing as both Josiah and the vicar stared on, looking ashen-faced and appalled. Josiah touched the vicar gently on the arm. 'I'm concerned about your health. Please rest. I will do my best to remonstrate with these poor misguided souls. Maybe God will send a sign. Otherwise the Lord Protector will visit as you mentioned.' The vicar took just a second to think about this before nodding sagely and turning in the direction of his house.

The vicar was still half-asleep when he heard voices close by. At first his mind drifted as it identified the voice of the tavern-owner. Then he heard the tavern-owner's wife. A red-faced sourpuss, thought the vicar, she surely drowns her sorrows. Idly, he thought that she didn't sound very happy. Then he heard the sound of another woman crying. Feet were scraping and shuffling up the path, and the voices became excited and more raucous. Quickly he roused himself and headed for the front door, just as his servant was in the process of answering it. With a quick curtsey, she showed him through the door, shutting it firmly behind him.

The vicar, confronted by quite a crowd gathering outside his house, stood dazed and unusually silent. A shocked-looking Josiah pushed his way to the front and, after a stuttering start, told the vicar how after he had left, the adults had begun to drift home with chores to do, leaving the children to play in the field. The children were playing leapfrog, which, of course, said Josiah, was not appropriate for the holy day. Josiah had therefore approached the children and asked them to play a different game.

'Why?' asked one boy insolently, 'Do you think the Devil himself will join in?' Returning to the game, the boy then repeated this to his friends with a great deal of bluster and swelling of his chest. All of the other children laughed raucously, slapping him on the back, oblivious to the fact that a spectator was watching their every move.

On any other day, if one of the boys glanced up at the tower of St Mary's church, they would see an archway about halfway up. It was an attractive building, although it was not particularly significant or important to the children. Yet none of the children were able to look at the tower or glance at it today. Some preternatural force meant that they could not look directly at the archway about halfway up the tower for more than a few seconds. The Devil himself was hiding there, as it was a comfortable position to watch the villagers misbehave.

Some of the boys thought they saw something unusual. There were flies buzzing around the archway and the top of the tower seemed to be engulfed in a thinning miasmic cloud. Yet as soon as they looked away they forgot what they had been thinking about in a way that was uncanny. They continued their game; their enthusiasm dinted not one iota.

Meanwhile, the Devil was idly surveying the landscape and reckoned that with his powers, he could reach the next field in one stride, and that, with a small skip, he could land on the top of a farm building. His mind wandered and he began to play with the thought of how he would take those boys, who had been playing the Devil's tune for weeks now, down into hell. Later, Josiah said he saw his own son, Jed, leaning forward to start another game of leapfrog when, with a whiff of sulphur, the Devil leapt down on to his back. The Devil clamped himself on to Jed's back and sprang into the air, hoisting Jed up with him as he rose into the sky.

Jed's screams were deafening and sick with fear, and Josiah raced through the long ears of corn with the rest of the children following him. He heard a thud and another scream. Following the sound of his son's cry for help, Josiah couldn't find him and realised that they must be in the air again. He reached the edge of the field, just as the Devil and the boy were plummeting down to earth.

Unable to move, Josiah watched as the rest of the children hurtled towards the pair. A huge hole opened up underneath his son and the Devil, and although the rest of the crowd drew to a halt, the ground disintegrated beneath them. Children attempted to claw at the soil, which was disappearing all around them, but they just found dust in their hands. In their terror, they realised that they were going straight to hell. With a pained expression, Josiah explained how the field had suddenly returned to normal. All that was left was a small stone about two-feet high, showing how the last child had been turned to stone.

The vicar stepped through the crowd of mourning parents as if carrying a heavy burden and asked Josiah to guide him to the spot. Not a word was said by anyone in the procession as they walked to the small stone and it was a bleak and subdued crowd who were addressed by the vicar when they finally arrived at the place that Josiah pointed out. The vicar sternly told the villagers that they had reaped their just reward. 'It is better that your children leave you now and spend some time in the Devil's company. If they are lucky, God will leave them there to understand their sinfulness but their young age may mean that they will eventually spend time with Our Lord. Any further time with you cursed sinners would have meant eternal damnation for their souls.' The wind whistled above them, interrupted only by the short hard call notes of a warbler. The message was stark and his flock had nothing to say. Little did the vicar know that his congregation already had plans for being reunited with their children and they were not going to wait until Judgement Day.

As Harvest Festival approached in October, the vicar looked on the churchgoers proudly, they had changed completely. It had been a hard lesson for these sinners but he knew that God worked in mysterious ways. The vicar did not see any need now to call on the Protector General Cromwell to show these families the error of their ways. He gazed fondly at a group of women who were praying quietly together at the end of the service with their heads bowed. All of them had their heads covered. At the back of the church he could see Josiah talking quietly to a group of men, they were planning how the church would be decorated with fruit and food at the time of the festival.

Truly, he thought, St Mary's had gone from a church to be ashamed of to a church to be proud of. He knew that the people bore the loneliness of being without their children and when families humbly approached him to ask if they could fill the empty space in their lives by taking in their nephews and nieces, he had to think hard. He was ready now to tell them what God had revealed to him.

The people of Marston Moretaine were also ready. Josiah had suggested to them that now was the time to put their plan into action.

Christmas found a sprinkling of children within the congregation. The vicar had said that the Lord in his magnanimity would allow the villagers to care for relatives. Josiah himself had a young boy with him and had revealed to the vicar how poverty had forced him to have Jed's twin brother fostered. Now that Jed had disappeared into the depths with the Devil, the family could afford to bring his twin back to the village. Josiah beseeched the vicar to pray with him to find God's will and the vicar was touched by the man's bovine acceptance of his fate. He may be a poor ignorant man, but he understood his place within God's firmaments. Josiah, meanwhile, was looking forward to returning the village to a place full of children and laughter.

As the New Year progressed, the villagers did sometimes play games and instruments but now they always did so away from the eyes of the vicar. More nephews and nieces, and young members of extended family came to stay at the village. The vicar had never taken a great deal of notice of the children, who tended to talk of childish things and wanted to play silly games. As long as the children were behaving, he barely registered which child belonged to which adult.

In fact if the vicar had looked closely he would have noticed very little change in the village from the year before. And if he had thought carefully, he would have looked at the stone with more than a passing interest. Was it really a naughty child that had been petrified? To him, the stone was an act of God to remind others what fate could befall them. A careful look would have shown that the stone carried the signs of thousands of years of storms, rain, sleet and sunshine. Left by our Stone Age ancestors, the stone had witnessed many events over the millennia. It had seen plague and pestilence, festivals and famine. It had been mute whilst anarchy had raged across the county and now the stone stood quietly as the villagers gradually brought their children back into the fold and made merry away from the eye of authority.

16

FINDING THE SOURCE

When they had first suggested it to him, he had shrugged the idea off – it was impossible to ask the gods for so much. Why risk their displeasure? Yet, the need for a ready source of water became more and more pressing. Whilst the elders tried to entice him into the venture with the suggestion that it would bring him a heroic status amongst his people, he felt that it was more likely a sacrificial act. If he survived and did not bring down the wrath of the gods then it would be a miracle.

By the time he approached the spot chosen by the holy men, his horse was moving leadenly. The clouds were thickening and the wind was beginning to whip up a storm. All of this seemed to suggest that the gods were against them. Reluctantly, he dropped from his horse, breathing deeply before beginning the incantations. Along with many of the Celtic tribes stretching across the seas, he felt a great respect for the god Lug, the bright one with the strong hand. He called on him to help him. As he placed an offering to the gods he felt a piercing pain in his right temple and dropped to the floor, clutching his forehead in pain. He started to retch as the light around him dimmed. Awestruck, he wondered if the power of more than one god was being brought upon him. When he attempted to stand and found his legs felt benumbed, he became ever more confused. Had the gods blocked out the light or was he now dying a slow and painful death of their choosing? Was he being taught a lesson for approaching the gods rather than waiting patiently for them? He lay for many minutes in a state of torpor waiting for the gods to finish him off.

The horse was nowhere in sight, obviously it had skittered away in fear whilst he retched on the ground. He found that he could crawl. The ground seemed to slope down and it seemed the path of least resistance to follow it. He felt every stone, every twig, every blade of grass on his journey's descent. Slowly he began to realise that although his body had been seized by pain, the aftermath had brought a sense of renewal. He was still weak but it was as if a coiled-up serpent had been awakened, stretching along his spine and heightening his senses. As the grass grew damp then sodden, his hands were tingling with the sensation of water. It was then that he began to feel the vibrations of the earth moving.

With juddering shakes, the earth seemed to disappear beneath him. He tried to scramble upwards, clods of sodden earth crumbled in his fingers. Utter darkness engulfed him as the weight of the earth started to descend upon him. Uselessly he tried to fend it off with his hands, willing himself to escape imprisonment. He tumbled downwards. Anticipating oblivion, the last thing he expected was to be touched. Yet that was what happened, he found himself wrapped in strong muscular arms. Then, feeling like a child, he truly did find oblivion as he collapsed in relief.

When he came to, he found himself next to flowing water. What was now a stream would over time become a river, the water cutting through the earth to create a riverbed. Tentatively he touched the water, it flowed through his fingers, gently caressing them. Murmuring thanks to the gods, he kissed the ground repeatedly. The gods had wrought their magic and had answered his prayers. He found the rocks and boulders from which the water flowed, venerating the place that would become sacred. The bubbles increased and then there was a surge of water, cresting,

curling and springing high above the ground. The light danced on the water's surface as it succumbed and fell back to earth.

The man stared into the water and saw the reflection of more than one face. The brightest eyes he had ever seen stared back at him and gave him a look so sharp that it brought to mind the memory of animals' throats cut in sacrifices. Not completely understanding what he was seeing, he winced and bowed his head. He did not know what was expected of him. Then he realised that the coruscating blue eyes were twinkling, and he was shaken by a roar that was laughter as his hair was tousled by a large friendly hand. As he turned, he caught sight of a bright armour-clad body moving through the spray. Later he would tell his family that he could not comprehend what he saw. He saw the god's muscular back and yet at the same time there was a face smiling back broadly at him. The god gave one last roar and raised his sword upwards. The man lost sight of him as he soared into the clouds.

Later the man would tell his kinsfolk that he had thought his mind was playing tricks on him. He began to realise, however, that he had truly seen a being with many faces both reflected in the water and as the god (for that is what the being was) ascended upwards. The man achieved a high status amongst his people as a holy man. As such he ensured that the spot from which the river had sprung was held sacred. The town built around the river was named after the three-headed god, thus it was called Lug's Ton. Or, as we may know it – Luton.

17

WITCHES

Elizabeth Pratt was seen as a burden by her village. The parish provided for her and she occasionally begged for 'ale and toast', but mostly people avoided eye contact and shuffled away when they saw her coming. Too many reminiscences, too much living in the past, had made her someone to be avoided. No one wanted to think back to the Civil War and no one wanted to hear about those she had lost. Everyone had their own misfortunes to bear.

Each morning she would rise early and eat a small chunk of bread for her breakfast, then she would tend her meagre patch of land, and after a lunch of pottage, potatoes and vegetables, she would wander around in the woods looking for herbs. She walked steadily, looking for chamomile, rosemary, balm and feverfew, using them to make ointments and cures she would sell to villagers. In the evening sometimes she had a meal, but often she did not.

Now everyone knew that when crops failed or water was poisoned, it was because amorous dragons had contaminated them. Although, of course, it was better not to mention that to the priest. And so when there was a poor harvest and the water smelt then gossip began. Well someone must have summoned the dragons, villagers would say with a knowing nod toward Elizabeth's hovel. Then one day, hawthorn was planted outside her door. It was a sign to everyone that saw it, a sign that said 'witch', and after that a number of villagers were afraid to look her in the eye.

Elizabeth kept up her daily routine, but now she was under scrutiny and villagers flinched when she offered them herbs from her daily rounds to help with scratches and scabs. Elizabeth was hurt and lonely but then she was used to being hurt and lonely. Not all of the villagers turned against her and some gave her a comforting pat on the shoulder or a shy smile. However, it may have been a smile that was her downfall. One day Elizabeth smiled at Thomas Heyworth's child and the next day the child was sick. Soon after she begged the barber surgeon, Josias Settle, for 'ale and toast', and when one of his children died she was taken in for questioning.

They accused her of witchcraft. John Smith, the local constable, stood over her and bent down towards her until his large, bulbous red nose was level with her own. Then he accused her of making contact with the Devil, of making young Henry Heyworth ill and of murdering young Charles Settle. In vain she protested that she loved the sweet little cherubs and that she would not harm a hair on their heads. But John Smith slapped her and arranged for her to be stripped to look for witch marks, finding a mole under her armpit. When they bought in young Henry Heyworth (the boy who had fallen ill when she smiled at him) to prick her with a pin, she found all her thoughts crowding in upon her. The doctors huddled round

discussing her while the child looked at her, his eyes wide with shock. Henry liked the old woman and did not want to hurt her, not even with a pin, but his very gentleness would seal her doom because the lack of blood 'proved' her witchcraft.

Water flowed all around her, pulling at her clothes and streaming into her mouth. It was murky and dark, and Elizabeth was strapped down. She could see the fronds of vegetation and it was only when she reached out to touch them that she realised that she was in a dream. She felt a pond loach slipping past her fingers and dug her hands into the sand as blackness surrounded her. As she came round her heart was racing and she could blearily make out horses' saddles hanging on the door and hay on the floor around her. She had obviously been locked in a stable overnight.

Two worlds collided in that moment and after that reality eluded her. For years, she had been isolated, aware that with more luck during the war, she would have been provided for by loving relatives rather than by begrudging charity. The shame of her dependence upon the villagers had weighed heavily on her. And now, the men she had seen as the bedrock of the community told her that she had hurt the boys. She started to doubt herself and imagined the scenes of cavorting on the top of the Dunstable Downs until it became real to her. Crying convulsively she admitted to anything that they charged her with. Yes, she said, she had met the Devil on Dunstable Downs and, yes, he had made a contract with her. He had promised that she would dress as well as the best woman in Dunstable. She had had three accomplices. The Devil ordered her to curse William Metcalfe's livestock and his pigs and many of his horses had died. She was half-crazed by now, her death an inevitability.

Witnesses, who wanted to enjoy some of the notoriety, claimed that she had vomited feathers, cotton, yarn, pins and two large waistcoat buttons. She was sent to Bedford Gaol but died before her sentencing. It was said that she had lost her wits completely by the time of her death. She had retreated in her mind to a safer, happier time and would hum country songs to herself, evoking soothing scenes from before the war. Her final words are said to have become a popular country song at the time:

> The fields and meadows are so green. As green as any leaf.
> Our heavenly father waters them with his heavenly dew so sweet.
> Our heavenly father waters them with his heavenly dew so sweet.

In Oakley around the same time, an elderly woman was accused by her neighbours of practicing witchcraft. She was alone, her husband had died and hardship had forced her children to move away. A meeting was held to decide her fate. She sat calmly, her hair grey and her hands heavily veined. She was told that in order to free herself from this accusation she must undergo the water ordeal or the parish officers could no longer help her. The officers had agreed to give her a guinea if she 'could clear herself by sinking'. It was this ordeal or starvation and so she had little choice. To prepare her for the water, she was tied up in a wet shirt, her thumbs and big toes were bound together, her cap was torn off and all her clothing was searched for pins. Her accusers believed pins would jeopardise any conclusion. The woman, petrified by shock, was impassive as they searched her.

She was dragged down to the river and in the moments before the ordeal, her eyes searched her surroundings. On top of a broad sweep of rolling hills stood a line of trees. On the other side of the River Ouse stood the church. The crowd grabbed the ropes and hauled her toward the water. The last thing she saw before she was pulled under the water was the frond of a daffodil tentatively revealing itself above the soil. As she raised her head above the surface of the water, spluttering and panicking, the crowd laughed and cheered. This was repeated again and again until a cry was uttered that as she had not drowned, then she must now be hanged as a witch. The crowd took up the cry whilst the woman lay bound and helpless on the ground next to the river.

Egged on by the baying crowd, one man rushed forward and kicked the woman, and at this a crowd surged towards her. She rolled up into a ball as they beat her, until one brave man stood in between her and the seething throng, appealing for calm and waving a Bible. He pleaded with the crowd to weigh her against the Church Bible, arguing that the Scriptures being the work of God must necessarily outweigh all the operations of the vassals of the Devil, and that if she were a witch then she would surely be of less worth (and weight) than the holy book.

When their weights were compared the woman was found heaviest and so innocent. This one man had given other men courage and a group reasoned with the crowd whose bloodlust was now up, allowing the woman to narrowly escape with her life.

18

Saint Christina

Christina was not the easiest person to serve faithfully as a servant, Hilda thought. Well maybe that wasn't entirely fair, Hilda loved her mistress and Christina was entirely selfless, but that was the problem. Christina's views about her calling in life meant that the two of them now found themselves here in a small corner of Bedfordshire in which Christina had chosen to spend each day in a cell.

Hilda looked down at her rough clothing as she fed the chickens and thought how differently it had all started. She had been with Christina's family, a noble Anglo-Saxon family, since she was little more than a child herself. There was a bond between herself and Christina, despite the difference in their station in life. So it was natural that Christina had insisted that she needed Hilda with her when she was travelling to St Albans, as well as a manservant to protect them. Of course, Hilda knew that she wanted to see more of the world than Huntingdon and was pleased to go along. Christina's father was a guild-merchant and provided Christina with under-dresses, over-dresses and headdresses of the finest fabrics for the trip. Hilda, meanwhile, wore coarse materials that rubbed against her skin and was expected to look drab and invisible compared to Christina who had clothes made from blue, green, yellow and violet.

This had never been a problem for Hilda. She had never had much and she never expected to have much. Loyalty to the family was something that her mother had drilled into her from an early age.

But how was she meant to be loyal to the family when their daughter, instead of looking forward to an advantageous marriage and the possibility of children, decided to make a vow at St Albans that was sure to cause chaos? Hilda berated herself for not noticing that something unusual was happening, but the fact was that she had been distracted. She had spent most of her time looking upwards in the abbey, thinking that she had found heaven shaped in stone, and became too engrossed in her own thoughts to think about Christina. Meanwhile, Christina had been on her knees, praying so hard that they must have become sore. When Hilda found Christina, praying with that sweet earnest look on her face and murmuring quietly to God, Hilda could not interrupt her. She started to wonder if her mistress perhaps had a sweetheart at home, she seemed to have so much to pray about. Yet that look on her face had been totally selfless and for a moment Hilda found herself closer to God just by being near Christina. Christina said she was very excited because she had made a vow but Hilda could not imagine what that vow could be.

It was obvious when Christina told her parents about her vow. There was a shriek that could have woken the dead – the rafters in the house shook and trembled with the force of it. Just as she could see a breeze passing through the rushes on the river, bending them and swaying them, Hilda knew how far the rumours about Christina had spread in the household. First there were the shared looks amongst those who attended to Christina's mother and father, then the whispered conversations that were hastily interrupted as she walked past. She knew the lower servants would soon be making coarse jokes at Christina's expense. Her parents had felt that they were kind to Christina in not finding a husband for her when she was fourteen. It was unheard of for a young woman of seventeen years to take a vow of virginity.

Hilda tried to stay as close to Christina's rooms as she could in the following days. Her parents would summon their daughter to their rooms and Christina would stand respectfully listening to them droning on for hours about their expectations of her, how she was created by God for motherhood and how that would be the only way that she could find fulfilment. Hilda allowed herself a couple of minutes to laugh up her sleeve when she heard that. As if Christina's father, who treated Christina like a valuable breeding mare, had any idea what the child faced. Christina spent many hours praying after she was summoned by her parents, asking God for guidance.

Christina was not the only one to ask for guidance, her parents were also considering their next move. For a while there was a lull in their campaign to discourage Christina from her chosen path. Christina even started to hope that they had accepted her vocation. Hilda, however, was far more suspicious by nature. Before very long Christina's parents made their next move.

This came in the shape of the flamboyant figure of Ranulf Flambard, who rode in on a thoroughbred horse, its coat shiny and its long sloping shoulders leading down to hindquarters that were strong and muscular. Tall and good-looking, his whole demeanour spoke of power and entitlement. He was the Bishop of Durham and the administrator of the Domesday Book. Hilda knew that Alveva, a townswoman, had been his mistress and they had had a number of children. Later he gave Alveva in marriage to another citizen of Huntingdon, and always lodged with her and her husband during his journeys from London to Durham and back. It was during one of these visits that he came to see Christina. The name Flambard meant devouring flame and from the way his hand hovered near Christina's waist when he spoke to her, Hilda thought that this was quite apt. Clearly Christina needed protection from Ranulf. Christina had always been kind to those who worked in the household and now those who had grown to love her saw any claims of piety from Ranulf as dubious in the extreme.

Hilda and a number of other servants worked together to ensure that someone was always close to Christina. On the second night of his visit, there was a knock on Christina's door. Hilda was sleeping on the floor and they both drowsily roused themselves from sleep.

Ranulf strode in and insisted that Hilda be dismissed from the room, with the implausible claim that he wanted to pray with her mistress. The two women shared a meaningful look as Hilda left; they had a plan for just such an eventuality as this. The pair had only been praying for a short while when Ranulf made his opening gambit, his hand reaching out to caress Christina's face tenderly. Christina held his hand in hers and murmured quietly that she was very nervous of a man's touch. She asked him to close his eyes as she undressed herself and waited for him in the bed. When he did so, she eased open her chamber door, quickly recovering her key, which was at the end of a ribbon hung round her neck, and locked him into her chamber. Hilda could only imagine how he reacted when he heard the door locking but when she unlocked the door the next day, he had a grim look on his face and left the house before nightfall.

The silence in the house between Christina and her parents became deafening. She was banished from society completely, not allowed to eat at the table with the rest of the household and not allowed to visit or receive visitors. Hilda found that where she had been Christina's servant, she became her gaoler, spending her day sitting outside her room to check that she did not find a way out and bringing her meals. At first Christina was quiet – praying and eating little. On the occasions that she got to see her, Hilda observed her carefully, fearing that the always-slight girl would become wraith-like.

Hilda was sitting outside Christina's rooms one day when her mistress's parents approached her; she felt her heart race and her mouth go dry as they walked silently towards her. Christina's father had dark circles under his eyes but his eyes were as sharp as a hawk's. Her mother looked as if she had been brooding on some imagined hurt. They ordered her to open the door and she could barely swallow as she mumbled back her response. Then their menacing presence was gone as they passed into Christina's room.

Soon the entire house knew that Christina's parents expected her to marry Burhtred, a friend of Ranulf Flambard. If Hilda expected Christina to crumble at this act of revenge as the forces of authority converged on her, then this was when Christina found her resilience. Hilda was relieved when Christina placed a letter in her hand for her to send to Robert Bloet, the Bishop of Lincoln. Despite all of the gathering forces against her, the child had found it within herself to fight. Although Hilda could not see why she wanted to take a vow of virginity, she wanted her to win not just this fight but also her battle to have a religious life. So each day she looked out of the window to see if a messenger arrived. When she heard that the bishop had agreed that Christina should not marry, Hilda did her best to hide how triumphant she was. This was just as well, as within weeks the bishop had been bribed and now changed his mind about Christina's need to marry.

If her parents had loved Christina once, Hilda saw little of it in the coming year. Their attitude towards her now hardened. And with the bishop now decided against her, Christina started to doubt her vocation. So many people were urging her to marry that in a moment of insecurity and claustrophobia, she agreed to a betrothal. A priest was called and the ceremony was conducted within the day. However, Christina refused to consummate the marriage and her parents saw this as a further problem to overcome. Shortly after the betrothal, her parents let Burhtred into her room at night, hoping that he would find her asleep and overcome her. He found her sitting on the bed, fully dressed. She chatted to him like a brother, telling him that she had been sent a vision by God and knew to expect him. She pleaded with him to live a life of chastity. The example of St Cecilia and her husband Valerian, who received crowns of chastity at their deaths, did not entice Burhtred. However, he did not have the heart to force the girl. Burhtred spent another hour with her, contemplating Christina's pure and angelic face as her conversation jumped from one example of a chaste life to another. When he finally crept out of her room, he was met by Christina's parents and their hangers-on. Grudgingly he had to admit that nothing had happened. As he left the room he heard laughter and the word 'spineless'. Unsurprisingly, her betrothed left the house soon after, returning to his home and promising to build a house for her near his father's house.

However, goaded on by his failure to seduce or force Christina, Burhtred soon returned to the house. Her father halted by the door just before unlocking it and turned to Burhtred saying, 'Do not be taken in by her deceitful tricks. She may look naïve but she is wilful and you must be manly. If you cannot do this on your own, call us and we will help you.' Straining to hear the voices, Christina was inside the room in her nightclothes. Cornered, her eyes swept up towards a small window seven-foot up and leading to a lengthy drop down on to cobbles below. She leapt on to the bed and sprang up towards the window, grazing her knees on the stone as she flailed wildly, trying to pull herself up. She fumbled with the latch and was pulling herself through the small gap to give herself up to a martyr's death on the stones below when Burhtred and her parents unlocked the door. Pulling her away from the window, she was dragged back into the room by Burhtred and her father.

Collapsing on to the floor, she kicked out like a feral animal, crawling towards her mother and throwing herself on her mercy, 'Please mother, be merciful'. At that, her mother, seemingly against her will, stepped aside and Christina struggled to her feet before running through the house. Doors opened as she tore through room after room and out into the coldest night of the year. Her father followed her. He pushed her into the middle of the courtyard, and struck her round the face, before stripping her of her nightdress. He returned to the house, ordering all of the servants not to let her back on pain of leaving his service in the morning. Outside, Christina's face bore a huge welt from her father's ring. At first she strove to cover her nakedness but then she knelt and prayed. As she prayed, there was a slight disturbance in the air and a whistle of the wind as a mist swept into the courtyard.

It left Christina as a spectral figure in its centre. Unseen servants threw blankets to Christina, which landed with a thump on the ground. She was found in the morning, smiling and sleeping like a baby, the blankets wrapped around her.

Hilda had never seen such cruelty in the house before and visited Eadwin, a local hermit, asking him to intercede on Christina's behalf. He visited the house as asked and, unsurprisingly, met with little success. Nevertheless, Hilda slipped from the house when he left and followed him through the woods as he journeyed back home. Eadwin quickly came to realise that she was in true earnest about the religious calling of her mistress. She told him pleadingly that she did not understand it but she knew when she was near someone who was close to God and that was Christina. The conversation stuck in his mind.

Days later, in the early hours of the morning, Christina was surprised to find the door to her room unlocked. Hilda greeted her with wide eyes and one finger placed over her mouth, shushing her into silence. Noiselessly they glided through the corridors, into the kitchen and out into the stable yard, the impenetrable dark gradually taking on an indigo hue as their eyes adjusted to the darkness. They stumbled to the stable where one of the lads had prepared horses for them. With quivering legs the young women mounted the horses and passed out of the gates to be enfolded into the woods just beyond them.

And that is how Hilda found herself in the care of an anchorite called Alfwen, as Christina's assistant. Eadwin the hermit had been so struck by his conversation with Hilda that he had organised Christina's escape and brought her to hide with Alfwen. Christina could not wait to begin her contemplative life. However, she needed the agreement of the bishop to do so and to ask for such agreement would reveal her whereabouts to her family. She also needed the support of another local hermit called Roger and appealed to him for patronage.

Roger, when threatened with the responsibility of a beautiful young girl, went fasting into his chapel. It took him two years to accept her as a charge. Christina lived those years in hiding. She lived a life of prayer but was unable to offer spiritual guidance. She received Holy Communion with Alfwen and in later years she would see it as a useful time to prepare her for what was to come.

Eventually the hermit Roger agreed to act as her patron. He moved her to a cell between Dunstable and Flamstead, nestled in a leafy corner of what later became Bedfordshire. But her trials were not over. To test Christina, Roger had her walled into such a small cell that she could hardly move. Hilda was shocked to see the conditions in which her mistress had to suffer in order to prove her religious calling. Cramped and restricted, she had one opportunity each evening to go out into the woods to answer the call of nature. Hilda felt close to tears when she saw what her mistress had to endure. She feared that if Christina became ill, she would never survive. Years in such conditions certainly affected her health yet Christina urged her assistant not to worry. She was following God's will.

After what seemed like an age, Roger began to trust Christina. Although Hilda had felt a great deal of animosity towards him for the way that he had tested her mistress, she started to relax in his presence and even smiled at him occasionally. Roger called Christina his Sunday daughter, 'myn sunendaege dohter', and Hilda felt her feelings towards him thaw completely when she saw the way he now doted on Christina and protected her. Roger called on Burhtred to release Christina from her betrothal so that her religious life, which she had led for so long, could finally be recognised. When Roger and Burhtred met, Hilda and Christina awaited news nervously. Only when Roger returned, waving a piece of paper signed by Burhtred and in the presence of a lawyer did they stop fretting. Christina could now commit herself fully to the Church.

Roger died shortly after Burhtred released Christina from her betrothal and it seemed only natural for Christina to take his place.

The years with Roger meant that Christina was now well respected by the local community for her spartan lifestyle. Most people saw only her eyes or her mouth through a small hole that was just big enough for her to give spiritual advice and counsel. Local people brought her problems ranging from how to tell their child that they could not afford an apprenticeship for them, to difficulties of illness and infirmity. Christina spent time praying with each of them and, as she encouraged them to open their hearts to God, many found the answer to their problems.

It was not only peasants and the common folk who respected her. The Abbot of St Albans trusted her advice. She was asked to take charge of a community of nuns at York but refused, saying that her place was with those earnest enough to seek her guidance as an anchoress. Then, when King Henry I died, the country descended into the chaos of a fight for succession between Matilda and Stephen. 'Lady Christina of the wood' provided an oasis of calm in the midst of such upheaval and she continued to administer to all who visited her, as well as to pray and to teach with her loyal servant next to her.

Eventually, Christina felt that the offer of prioress of a community of Benedictine nuns was what God wanted for her. Behind the scenes, the Abbot of St Albans, who had relied on her advice, and the Dean and Chapter of St Paul's Cathedral in London also, had arranged this offer for her. She ended her days in peace, with Hilda close by, loved by everyone she had touched, from the most humble to the most exalted.

19

LEATHER BREECHES

The sign of the pub swayed in the wind and leaves tumbled down the deserted street. Travellers were welcomed by the clank of a bell and the sight of a bright open fire as they came in from the cold. Thomas Odell's smile as he ushered in travellers was warm and unforced. He ran what was known as a shebeen, a place that was unlicensed. They were usually associated with disreputables, criminals and people who only just managed to keep on the right side of the law.

Thomas's establishment was plain but welcome and as shebeens went it was respectable. It catered for many of the men making bricks in Wootton. The fare was bread and meat, and the rooms were drab but comfortable. However, the man had so much blather and good-natured prattle that guests felt at home and took a delight in the sincerity of their host. His place was well liked and recommended. Even so, Thomas and his wife struggled, and he had to work on Sundays mending ditches. It meant rising early and he imagined, as he strode down the lane early on a Sunday morning, that the curtains were twitching to catch a sight of him in his leather breeches. He loved Rosie, his wife, and was faithful to her, but he knew that he was still attractive to the female eye. As his hips swayed in those breeches, he relished the moment.

One winter, the snow was so high that all but the most reckless stayed at home and ate what provisions they had. There was no way that they could travel from Wootton into Bedford to buy more food, even if they had the money. The sun shone over the fields, and the reflection was stark and almost blinding. The whiteness stretched over to the horizon, interrupted by the crude shapes of tree branches. And the snow was still coming down. When they had eaten almost all the provisions they had, Rosie and Thomas took to their bed and dreamed of hogs, bogs, fairies and witches. They were woken by a loud noise at the front door. Hurriedly, Thomas shoved on his breeches, raised his window and, with a bravado he did not feel, shouted, 'What is going on down there?'

Paddy McGurk, with a voice as rich and dark as Turkish coffee, replied, 'Now Thomas all we're wantin' is some grub.' And a voice which Thomas knew belonged to Andy Moore hollered, 'We'll burst open your door, Thomas. If you don't give us some food, we'll rip off your breeches, we've all seen you swaggering around in them.' At this, despite their hunger, there was much mirth and sniggering. Even though they were good-natured now, Thomas knew how a crowd could turn. He made for the door and took the stairs two at a time so that he arrived at the bottom just in time to see the door bursting open and the mob rushing in. They crowded around Thomas like moths to a flame and he had to use the best of his blether to convince them that he would serve up all that his shebeen had to offer.

Thomas felt a sharp pang of worry as he ran up to his bedroom. The words came tumbling out to Rosie, 'All starvin'. No food. They'll be trouble if we don't give them something.' And then there was a long moment as they stared at one another, convinced that their troubles were about to turn into a catastrophe. Thomas glanced down at his breeches, 'They said they'd have the breeches off me, if I didn't feed them.'

'Well if they don't mind their meat a bit tough,' said Rosie with a snort and then stared at Thomas with a calculating look, her eyebrows raised speculatively.

'That's it, Rosie my love!' Thomas cried and hugged her quickly.

They rushed around the house, finding a dried-out old onion in the back of a cupboard, a few wizened carrots in one of the out-houses and food that they had kept back to eke out over the next week. They started to make a stew. Thomas held a knife to cut up the breeches and his hand hesitated for just a moment. The breeches reminded him of his younger days with Rosie. He had enjoyed the way women's eyes swept over him appraisingly. He looked at Rosie. She was feisty and fun, and she had never lost any of her lustre to him. His hidden bit of vanity was nothing compared to keeping Rosie safe. In his haste to placate the men below, he almost clawed out the stitches, buttons pinging off the dour walls of their bedroom. He cut the breeches into strips, hoping that the men would seize on them as pieces of tasty offal. Then he boiled them until he saw signs that they were starting to soften.

Soon the smells of the stew wafted into the bar, helped by Thomas using the door like a bellows, with the excuse that it had a dodgy hinge. Those poor men were so hungry that the smell of some wrinkled carrots, onions and cabbage made their stomachs yearn for the wonderful meal awaiting them. Fearful of what the men would do if they grew wise to the ruse, Rosie had flitted away into the night to escape any potential trouble. To give her more time, Thomas had brought out the best plates and cutlery. The door into the bar was opened with a flourish and the men now expected the rich succulent taste of mutton or beef.

'This is what we've been waiting for,' said Barney, ladling a generous portion of the stew. He speared a chunk of the breeches with a fork and muttered, 'You're no judge of mutton,' as he chewed and chewed.

'Aye,' said Andy, 'this is tough.' And silence descended as all of the men concentrated on the task in hand of filling their stomachs.

'Hold up,' cried Brian, 'I thought this was fat.' Reaching into his mouth with his finger, he hooked out something small and hard. Indignant and hungry he stared at it, 'What's this?' he asked, as liquid dripped off of it and the shape began to emerge of a small white button with one small hole in the centre. As he held it up, it seemed to blink ominously at Thomas, who took a step backward towards the door. Brian fell to his knees and screeched, 'We've been trying to shove our teeth through Thomas's old breeches!'

The men rose as one, turning towards Thomas. In the silence, Thomas talked giddily, 'All we could find in the cupboard, lads. No harm done, you see.' He stopped. Brian moved towards him and then veered off towards the table. 'Pray send for the priest, for surely I've been poisoned.' He raised a plate high above his head and then sent it crashing down to the floor. Thomas fled from the house. As he pulled open the latch of his gate, he heard the sounds of pottery shattering and chairs splintering. He slipped into the woods and listened as the men took their revenge. They broke plates, pots, pans, chairs and dishes; all the time searching the house for the food that he knew wasn't there. As he suspected, the men were hungry enough to break things, but not angry or malicious enough to set his home on fire.

In the months after the snow, everybody was much thinner. Thomas repaired the chairs and patched together what he could. He realised that hunger will drive men to do things that they would never normally do. When the men from that night sheepishly returned to the shebeen, he gave them small smiles, letting them pretend that it had just been a bit of an argument. He and Rosie were safe and everyone had just enough money to eat. He knew that he had to be satisfied with that. Thomas never did have enough money to buy another pair of leather breeches, but as Rosie did a good job of keeping him warm at night, he didn't really mind.

In the Chequers Inn pub in Wootton, which took the shebeen's place, tales have been recounted of glasses falling from shelves when no one had touched them. At quiet times in the inn, staff sometimes see a reflection of a face in the Pint Pots. No matter how quickly they turn, however, there is nobody there, just the sound of distant laughter.

20

THE GIANT OF THE FIVE KNOLLS

Once there were giants. None of the humans were going to challenge a giant who could pulverise them without a second thought and, as a result, the giants roamed over our island with impunity. What made it even worse was that most of the giants were spiteful. They were bitter, unforgiving, petty and prone to holding grudges. They usually resorted to violence, often against their own kin, and it was not uncommon to find a dead giant slumped over a mountaintop.

The people who lived on the edge of this constant violence and treachery knew to stay unnoticed. Sometimes they would find the dead body of a giant, killed by a rival, sprawled over their farmland. People covered their faces with scarves as the stench of the body started to attract flies. Even in their shelters the fetid smell of decay was impossible to escape and the people thought the constant fear of starvation or a violent death would never end.

With their bitter fights and enmities, the giants' numbers gradually declined. One of the giants declared himself king but that just made it worse as other giants plotted to topple him from power. The feuding spiralled out of control until there were just a few lonely giants living as hermits and a scattering of half-giants who lived amongst the people in relative harmony. In Dunstable, the people felt themselves both lucky and unlucky. It was unlucky to have not one giant but

two, but then again, at least these two were in love. They just hoped that the union wouldn't result in offspring. The giant Bolster was a colossus. He could stand with one foot in Dunstable and the other in Luton – a distance of about five miles. The love of his life was called One-Eye and she was just as physically impressive.

The two giants lumbered across the landscape hand in hand, looking into each other's eyes. Although they usually avoided flattening houses, if a sheep got in the way then the result was a woolly bloody blot on the landscape. When they had an argument it was much worse – rocks were thrown and valleys were created as a giant jumped up and down, trembling with fury.

After a particularly bitter row, the townspeople of Dunstable got together, they wanted all of the rocks and the rivers and the houses to stay in the same place. And so a delegation of the menfolk went to talk to Bolster, taking with them huge cows that had been roasted on a spit as a peace offering and a massive cup fashioned so that Bolster could easily scoop water from a lake. Placating him until he sat down and ate with them, they sympathised as he poured out his troubles. At the same time a delegation of the womenfolk went to talk to One-Eye. Cautiously, as she had threatened to stamp on them, they soothed her and some of them even felt sorry for her. She told them that her and Bolster were actually a bit weedy by giant standards and had been teased. Humans and half-giants alike dreaded to think what the rest of her race were like and many thought that they would simply cower under a rock if one turned up.

After their talk with the two giants, life carried on much more quietly. Occasionally someone visiting the well would need to creep past a sleeping giant with the giant's hot breath pouring down their neck, but the people of Dunstable felt that they had peace. True, it was an uneasy peace, but it was better than the chaos of their distant past and the uproar of their recent past. This peace was to be broken, however, when a part of Bolster and One-Eye's past came to find them.

The sound reverberated like a hunting horn, huge and booming. The buildings shook with the force of it and, as the people peered out of the houses, they thought a new mountain had appeared. Their faces were pinched as they stared up into the sky and gradually made sense of the great bulk in front of them, which was now bellowing, 'Bolster!' The branches in the trees were thrown back and the leaves rippled violently with the force of it. Even the insects were scurrying away in fear.

The chief almost fainted with shock. First he was woken up by a huge voice resonating throughout his house. Then when he tried to walk out of his door, he was confronted with a six-foot-wide eye. It was surprisingly a thing of beauty. A luminously clear blue pupil, with the white of the eye flecked and contoured.

The eye belonged to Bolster, who hissed (as quietly as a giant can hiss), 'We've got to do something. Bob has come to see me. Don't like me very much.'

Perplexed, the chief asked, 'Who's Bob?'

'We went to school together. I got really pop'lar when I called him pus-face. Everyone copied me and he's hated me since. I'm scared. 'E's nasty.'

At this a huge tear slowly welled up at the base of the eyeball and the chief watched it slipping down to the floor. 'What on earth do you suggest we do?' asked the chief, thinking that if he hadn't had the wits scared out of him already then he would be beside himself with fear by now.

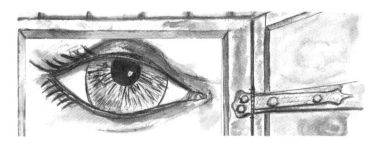

'One-Eye is hiding behind the woods,' said Bolster, blinking rapidly. 'Errm,' he stumbled to a stop. It was clear that this was as far as his plan had got. The chief was used to being in charge, even though ordering around giants wasn't something he had done before. 'We'll send a messenger. Sing, she needs to sing. Then we'll work with you, Bolster. I've got an idea.' It wasn't the best plan ever but it would have to do.

The messenger was rather wary of being seen by this new aggressive giant and took a much longer and more indirect route than was really necessary in order to reach One-Eye with the message to sing. Finally, however, the sound of a huge cacophonous din swelled across the landscape, 'When I'm calling you, oh ohhh ohhh'. The singing was mercifully interrupted by a round of coughing, but it had done its job and attracted Bob's attention. Bob had been looking in the other direction, but when he heard One-Eye, he wheeled round and lurched towards her. He raised the club that he had been leaning on into the air and now the iron spikes protruding from its surface were visible to all. The giant advanced towards her at a speed that no one had thought him capable of and reached down to pull her up from her hiding place by her hair. As he pulled her upright, she screamed.

Bolster forgot about the plan, he forgot about the club with iron spikes and he forgot about his own safety. He bellowed and, with a rush of courage that he would never have had for himself, he launched himself on to Bob's back. One-Eye stopped screaming and fainted. Bob flailed around with his club, the spikes grazing One-Eye before he dropped it and it clattered loudly to the ground. In the chaos, the humans crawled out of their hiding place in Bolster's hair and any semblance of a plan disappeared as they dangled from strands of hair, using any tools that they had to scratch, pierce and inflict pain on Bob. At this close range to Bob, Bolster now knew with absolute certainty that Bob had not washed for at least a month.

'Come on! Come on!' yelled the chief, and a group of his men carrying logs of wood, slipped down to Bolster's shoulders and launched themselves at Bob, catching hold of Bob's unruly mop of hair and swinging there precariously. Bob threw his head back, flinging the logs into a trajectory up into the air. When he swung his head back down, the logs took a graceful arc through the air and curved straight into Bob's nostrils. Bob could take no more, he roared and thundered across the landscape, desperate to escape. He stopped only briefly to flick off some of the humans, who landed on the top of the trees in the nearby wood. When they climbed down, they were amazed to find that nobody was hurt.

The two giants and the humans returned to Dunstable, and the giants were shocked to find that a feast had been prepared for them. Before they knew it, children were clambering up on to their shoulders to kiss their cheeks and ineffectually cuddle them. The giants had previously accepted presents, but these had been offered as a way of buying friendship. Real friendship is, of course, different. There are some things that once you share, you cannot help but become friends. Fighting a villainous and seemingly invincible giant with multiple personality issues is one of them.

The next few days were full of celebrating. One-Eye was subdued and tired but she enjoyed watching the little people dance. Slowly, however, it became apparent that she was not regaining her health. The slight graze from the iron spikes had never healed and the people realised that the tips must have been poisoned in some way to be causing such sickness. The giant was fading fast. The townspeople did everything they could to keep Bolster calm and to help his lady friend get better. It was difficult to know how to treat a giant and Bolster's tears created new rivers. They kept Bolster busy by asking him to fetch herbs from the Shetlands or Brittany. When he returned he would watch them prepare huge poultices.

One day, when her temperature was particularly high, all of the humans and half-giants were so busy with One-Eye that they didn't even register the earth shuddering as Bolster walked across the landscape, halting to sniff back his tears and drag a dirty sleeve across his tear-stained and rather snotty face. Abruptly, everybody stopped as they heard a crack rent the air. Bolster had run head first into an oak tree. But instead of reaching oblivion as he had hoped, he just developed a nasty headache. Soon they heard the sound of rocks being pulverised. When Bolster shambled back, the humans shook their heads sadly. There was nothing they could do to ease his pain and One-Eye didn't have more than a few moments left to live.

After One-Eye had breathed her last, Bolster looked down at her body, which had been wracked with pain. In a voice thick with emotion, he said, ''Ank you for looking after my One-Eye. She couldn't 'ave asked for better friends.' Later that night, the air charged with grief, the people and half-giants of Dunstable heard a storm rumbling in the distance. Or maybe it was the sound of a giant's muffled sobbing, it was difficult to tell.

In the years to come, the people of Dunstable looked after their giant, making sure that he was never lonely. He, in return, did his best to look after them – they never went hungry if the harvest was poor and they never lacked materials for erecting new houses when necessary. When he reached old age, Bolster asked them to bury him in the land that he had come to love. He was laid on the ground and his hands were crossed on his chest as he had instructed. When they had succeeded in covering him with earth, it was apparent that he had changed the landscape completely. Where the land had been flat, there was now a ridge. The people did their best to show their respect for the giant and he was remembered in special ceremonies along with other ancestors. Yet even the clearest memories drift away like a scent in the wind.

Whatever the weather, the people of Dunstable will stride up to the top of the ridge. Standing by one of the five mounds or knolls, you can survey much of the surrounding countryside. Occasionally a kite, catching one of the thermals in the wind, will float past imperiously with a slight flutter of its tailfeathers. The five knolls are one of the most beloved features of the Bedfordshire countryside. The giant, who loved this county, would probably be happy to know how many people enjoy those knolls, unaware that the giant's hands lie beneath them and the knuckles of one hand form the outline of the knolls.

This is one of a number of myths about the Five Knolls. Another tale suggests that the knolls are the burial place of five kings. The Five Knolls actually consists of not five but seven barrows and it is the best example of a round barrow cemetery in the Chilterns. In excavations in 1928, archaeologists found a crouched female skeleton with a Neolithic knife in a grave pit in the central barrow. Later, in Saxon times, about thirty bodies were buried here in rows, with their hands tied behind their backs, leading to speculation that they were victims of a massacre. Centuries later, the site was used as a site for gallows and historians suggest that the bodies of those that were hanged were buried where they fell.

21

Murder in
Flitwick Woods

It was a cold grey day in late November and Joseph Cooke was leaving the cottage of Elizabeth White. Smugly he thought he'd given a simple girl a little bit of earthly pleasure to brighten her day. It never crossed his mind to worry about her reputation or to wonder how she managed to provide a home and food for herself and her young boy aged four years old. When she saw the look on the face of her next-door neighbour, Martha Dawborn, the next day whilst beating her rugs, Elizabeth was at pains to point out that she had not known any other man but Joseph Cooke since her boy, William, was born. Her neighbour tried to keep her face as still as a stone. Back in her cottage, Martha could not keep herself from thinking that Elizabeth White had known a fair few before the boy's birth but she liked Elizabeth and kept her own counsel.

After the excitement of a visit from Joseph Cooke, Elizabeth now returned to the drudgery of making lace. Her two sisters had returned to the cottage when Joseph Cooke's visit had finished. A little bit of visiting neighbours and washing laundry had given the couple some privacy. Both sisters were concerned that if Elizabeth had another child and Joseph Cooke did not accept it as his, then the parish would start to resent the one shilling and sixpence paid from the rates to support the single mother. The last thing that the family needed was moralising visits from their elders and betters.

Without the stability of a man's wage, life for the three sisters and the little boy was insecure. The income from lace was pin money, seen as a way of adding to a family's income rather than a living in itself. Elizabeth and her sisters lived a precarious existence, finding small pleasures in each other's company and occasionally in a visit to the alehouse and the physical comfort of a man's company. Inured to a life of poverty, they never knew how much money they would have left by the end of the week and thought carefully about what they had to buy.

Their world was a small one, centred around the parish. The only way for folk to get around was by horse, in a carriage if you were rich and at the back of a pony trap if you were poor. They did not want to leave this small world. The sisters dreaded the parish finding a reason for moving them to another neighbourhood or the poorhouse. Their fear was that the last sight that their neighbours would have of them would be leaving for a poorhouse far away. They had seen it happen to others, members of a family bundled into the back of a pony trap with a few paltry possessions.

Joseph Cooke was from a family of bakers. He had never worried about money. He looked after his wife, his children and his employees well. At least, nobody had said anything to the contrary to him. After some years of bearing and caring for children, his wife's face was starting to lose its rosy lustre and she had a hawkish look about her, as if she was readying herself for the next request for better clothes, china dinnerware and silverware. Life felt tedious and spiritless without visits to women such as Elizabeth. Sarah Line was his charwoman and at least some of her seven or eight children were his. He was a bit tight-lipped if anyone tried to find out if there were more women.

Joseph did not love Elizabeth any more than Elizabeth loved Joseph. They did, however, find some pleasure in each other's company. Elizabeth also relied on Joseph's small presents of money, which made visits from the merchant she sold her lace to more bearable. The merchant would always wince at some minor fault in her lace and gave her as little money as he could get away with. Nevertheless, Elizabeth knew that her choices were to take his pittance or find some factory work. She'd seen the blank faces of the people who worked in a factory. They must rise each day with bells to regulate their comings and goings, and at the day's end, prepare themselves to do the same again the very next day. You even had to ask the foreman's permission to answer a call of nature! No, she would avoid that if she could. She had the fields nearby and her son close to her. So she bobbed a curtsey and spoke politely to the merchant, and spat in the drink she made him.

Now Joseph was starting to find his enjoyment of these visits to Elizabeth dimming. He had, at some level, enjoyed the subterfuge and the secrecy, and the need to lie to his wife. It had added to the anticipation of his visits to Elizabeth. By the time she had started to undo the ties on her corsets, he was almost overcome with lust. Later he felt peaceful and sleepy, and her chatter was like birdsong, a backdrop to his feeling of well-being. Now his visits were part of everyday life. The neighbour even nodded to him as he left the cottage. And the way Elizabeth prattled on so about the merchant and the price he paid for lace!

A couple of days later, he was looking over his accounting books. He closed the books and, grabbing his greatcoat, strode off to meet Elizabeth in the woods. In the past, meeting in such a place, with the slight possibility of one of the gentlemen of the town finding him, had added a certain frisson to the encounter. Now he found it all very predictable. Just before they parted, he gave Elizabeth a sixpence saying, 'This must be one of our last meetings, Lizzie. If anyone finds out it will be difficult for me. You must see that.'

He looked down at her overbearingly, without a hint of fondness. 'I'll meet you here tomorrow so you can return my watch.' At that he walked away, proud that he had started to extricate himself from the affair. Elizabeth stared after him, not sure what to make of this sudden change in tone.

Elizabeth didn't go to the meeting. She didn't see how it would serve her or how she could leave it with any dignity. She found his protestations of a difficult life bewildering and didn't want to hear them. Later he appeared at the cottage door, demanding his watch. She let her sisters talk to him and made him wait while she arranged her clothing and hair to catch his interest. She saw the inner conflict. His face flushed as she smiled at him and toyed with a pendant hung on a string of lace resting on her breast.

When he finally got to talk to her alone he looked unhappy. His brow furrowed as he cursed himself for the weakness of wanting her and he found himself blurting out a suggestion to meet. They arranged to meet the next morning. Elizabeth did not know why she felt a feeling of victory. She could not say that she loved or respected the man. She was used to being desired but never valued; yet she did not want to be discarded so easily. Complicated feelings meant that she sought to attract him back to her when he had also begun to repulse her. They parted with a kiss.

On the Monday morning of their meeting, Elizabeth stared thoughtfully into the fire. She had had a small breakfast and felt the knot of anxiety in her stomach tighten at the thought of the meeting to come. She dressed plainly, unsure of the impression that she wanted to make, tucking her hair into a cap. As she stepped out of the cottage, the early morning mist was starting to thin out. She could see how the frost gilded the ivy. As she walked through Ampthill, she pulled her cape up and around her face. As the time of the meeting drew closer she was seen by Henry Cooper and a little later by Thomas Cooke (who shared a surname but no kinship with Joseph Cooke) on the north–south path through Flitwick Wood. Later Henry Cooper would say that she was not herself. Thomas Cooke would remark on how distracted she was, oblivious to her surroundings and barely giving him a nod of acknowledgement. She usually looked around keenly, happy to catch a sight of the deer that lived in the forest or maybe a wren amongst the undergrowth.

Joseph, of course, did not prepare his breakfast but he was also thinking of other things. Forgetting that he himself had suggested the meeting, he had started to wonder why he was obeying Elizabeth's bidding. To his mind, his life seemed to be ruled by her capriciousness. Gripping hold of the breakfast knife, he brooded on his vain attempts to end the affair. She had taken no notice and he could not fathom whom he loathed the most, her or himself. He had expected to feel in control when she had returned the watch, yet now he found himself playing to her tune once again. As he sliced through the meat laid out for breakfast, he was mesmerised by the power of the knife in his hand and a dark idea began to form in his head. He slipped the sharp knife for the meat into his coat pocket. It was one of a set and later that day his wife would wonder how it had been misplaced. The knife, now in his coat pocket, fitted snugly next to his clasp knife. He then went to the toolbox in the corner of his house and picked up a hammer. Without saying a word to his wife or servants, he left the house.

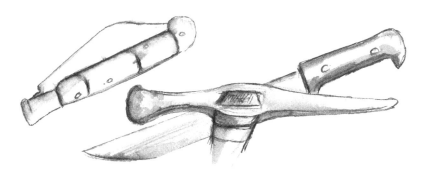

As Joseph Cooke walked to Flitwick Wood, his rage grew in intensity. Taking no heed of who he met or how he looked, he hurried through the woods clutching the hammer. The winter sunlight reached the forest floor and Joseph Cooke took no notice. A nuthatch flew above him, looking for food, and Joseph Cooke took no notice. When he saw John Osborne, he was still holding the hammer. He was thinking only of what he would do to Elizabeth when he met her.

Elizabeth was waiting by their favourite tree. As Joseph approached her, Elizabeth could see an intensity in his eyes. Revulsion at his own inadequacies and her craven desire to keep him at any cost to her dignity had given him a purpose. Up till now, that purpose had been only to frighten her. He raised his arm with the hammer above her head. Her eyes widened with shock, but something inside him was triumphant at her silent reaction to his display of power. She shied away from him and the thought passed through his mind that he would hold ultimate power over her if he hurt her. How good would that feel? And then, before he realised what he was doing, blow upon blow rained down upon her. Upon the back of her head and then upon her face.

Elizabeth fought back as best she could but she gradually weakened and fell to the ground, staring up at Joseph in terror. Panicking and only now realising what he had done, Joseph took out the breakfast knife and cut her throat. As he leant back upon the oak tree that had until now been a place of sweet memories, he looked at her dead body and wished that what had been done could be undone.

A madness overtook him now and Joseph tried to tidy up the scene. He gathered Elizabeth up into a ball, so that she would look to a passer-by as if she was sleeping. He collected his hammer, unaware that he had left both his breakfast knife and his clasp knife next to the body. Terrified that he could no more make himself look innocent than he could reverse the course of time, he fled.

As he ran he took off his jacket and wrapped the jacket round the hammer. He told himself that if anyone saw him, he could simply say that he had walked far and no longer needed his jacket. As he put a distance between himself and Elizabeth's body, he became calmer. If he could just reach home without seeing any of his neighbours, then he would say that he had finished with Elizabeth long ago and that she had another lover.

Joseph Cooke was seen by many of his fellow villagers on the way home. When Elizabeth's body was discovered the next day, constables found one of his kitchen knives and a clasp knife close to her body. His arrest was inevitable. At the inquest, Joseph made many attempts at defence, each of them preposterous and utterly implausible. When presented with the breakfast knife and clasp knife, he showed a new clasp knife that he had bought at Ampthill Fair. He said he had given his bloody clothes to a servant to be laundered and protested that the blood on his lapels was from rabbits that he had killed. The next day he was taken from a local lock-up to Bedford Prison where he stood trial the following year and would be hanged.

On the same day as the inquest, Elizabeth White was given a pauper's burial attended by her sisters and her young son. The service was short and the family soon returned to their home to pick up their lives. Elizabeth had been beautiful, yet year upon year the memories of her faded. Her son grew up knowing that whispered conversations would suddenly turn silent as he came nearer. It was not easy being the son of a murder victim, just as it was not easy being poor. His two aunts were often distracted by poverty and the burden of trying to keep him fed and healthy. The moments of affection they did show him were soothing, and he enjoyed the happy times that they described of his mother as a young girl with him as a small boy. He found himself remembering brief glimpses of her but he was unsure if these were real or imagined. When he grew up and moved away from Ampthill, the last lingering traces of Elizabeth White disappeared for ever.

22

Dorothy Osborne

The carriage shook from side to side as it hit yet another hole in the road. All of the travellers began to grumble. A stout woman in flowing brown clothing remarked to no one in particular that she had the sorest arse in Christendom and outside they heard the sound of the whip as it cut like a razor through the air and the thud as it landed on the horse's back. In one corner of the carriage, Dorothy Osborne struggled to repress a smirk and she did her best to catch her brother's eye in the corner furthest from her.

Henry found her irrepressible. Their childhood at Chicksands Priory had been idyllic, living in the remains of a Gilbertine cloister surrounded by acres of land. Now he needed her sense of adventure to keep him sane, as they tried to escape England in the grip of a bitter civil war. Dorothy's irreverence and sense of fun lit up her face and made her hugely attractive. As she started to doze off, despite the discomfort of the carriage, she seemed to be a fairly ordinary young woman with a long and angular face. In conversation she was mesmerising.

Waking, Dorothy adjusted her cape and tucked her hair into her bonnet. She did her best to assume the attitude of a truly god-fearing soul who detested theatre and dancing. Her brother looked over as she fought to keep a grin from her face. She knew that he felt she would have a much better chance of succeeding in life if she could keep her abundance of energy and mirth under control.

Last year, the New Model Army had been formed and a couple of months ago, King Charles had surrendered to the Scots. Dorothy's family were Royalists and, along with her brother, she had taken to the road to escape retribution from the Parliamentarians and to join their father, once the commander in Guernsey, who had retired to St Malo in France.

When they arrived at the Isle of Wight, held by Parliament, they did so without anyone discovering their identity or their loyalties. Their ship was due to sail in a day, forcing them to spend an extra day on the isle. They meandered around the port, briefly stopping to watch the shipbuilders. Dorothy squinted as she looked up into the sun as the mast was raised on the ship. A huge hole gaped at the back, ready for planks to be fitted. She could smell the cloying, sweet yet repulsive smell of boiling tar further along the harbour and could hear children playing and splashing each other.

As they headed further into town to get provisions, a coach swerved towards them, narrowly missing them. Heading into the relative safety of a narrow alley, sailors and soldiers sidled past them, jostling their boxes without apologising. The upper stories of the buildings seemed to be tottering above them and their movements were hampered by pedlars accosting them to buy flowers, food, beads, knives and cloth. Eventually they reached their destination and their evening was spent lying low in the inn, keeping to their rooms. Henry was talkative and good company, although Dorothy sometimes felt he had a complacent attitude to life. He liked to fit in with whatever friends he had at the time and take the easy route. She settled down to sleep as Henry joked about skulking around in dark corners and didn't notice when he used his diamond ring to scrawl some graffiti about the Parliamentarian governor.

The sails were unfurled and the last few boxes had been heaved on to their ship when the soldiers came for them. A grim-looking captain asked Henry where they had been staying and in which rooms. Keeping the jitters in her stomach under control, Dorothy strode up to him.

'Can I help you, Captain?' she asked in a low voice.

He threw her a look, clearly thinking her impertinent, and continued talking to her brother.

'Did you touch or mark anything in your room?'

'I don't know what you are talking about,' Henry replied in clipped tones, but the aristocratic, confident voice belied his schoolboy manner. She knew him well enough to know that his evasiveness hid guilt and he cast her a quick apprehensive glance.

If care was taken loading their boxes on to the ship, none was shown in the unloading. Now that they were an obstacle to setting off, sailors pelted along the deck, boxes were thrown on to the jetty, scarves and jewellery strewn on to the quay in the process. Dorothy was escorted away and she turned around to look at her brother.

His arm was held tightly behind his back and he shook his head imperceptibly to warn against her saying any more.

A day later, Henry was in jail. As a gentlewoman, Dorothy had spent a day in the household of Colonel Hammond, who would be responsible for a decision in their case. She kept the mood light but steered the conversation towards the cause of Henry's imprisonment. The colonel tapped his pipe on a side table and coughed importantly as he imparted the news that they had discovered writing about the governor scratched under the window.

Dorothy uttered her dismay, clutching her handkerchief to her chest to show the shock and horror expected of a respectable woman. Her thoughts were racing as she asked whether it was – wrongly, of course – believed that her brother had made these markings and whether they thought he was professing loyalty to the king. The colonel looked at her despondently, shaking his head and saying that it was more personal than that. Dorothy immediately knew that her brother was likely to lose his life and there was little she could do about it.

As she tried to sleep, Dorothy thought of the many happy memories of their childhood at Chicksands Priory. She had enjoyed long walks in the countryside. Sometimes she had returned at sunset to see the countryside imbued with a golden light and the house glowing with the light from the sunset and the fires that servants were beginning to light. Back then her brother had been one of the most important people in the district. Now this war meant that a man's life was cheap. It could be snuffed out as easily as a candle. She continued to fret during the night and only fell asleep in the early hours.

The next day, Dorothy was allowed to attend her brother's hearing. A clerk ushered her to a seat and she sat in silence, brooding on her next move. People wove around her, relaying messages to the colonel in soft tones and bringing papers to his desk. Eventually her brother was brought in. They stared at one another, knowing that the beginning of the end was imminent. Then the colonel called everyone to attention, crying 'Gentlemen' before, with a nod in her direction, adding, 'and lady'.

His next remarks summarised the case and, as he drew to an end, Dorothy rose, gathered her skirts around her and interrupted him with a delicate, 'Excuse me, Sir'. Then in a tremulous tone, she declared that she could explain everything, that she had overheard some men talking and laughing, and that she had used a ring to mark the wall herself. Of course, she was oblivious to the real meaning of what she was copying. For a moment everyone in the room was thunderstruck and then, like the dawn chorus, the noise gathered and gathered as everyone in the room began to discuss her version of events.

'Quiet please,' snapped the colonel and a hush settled as he looked sternly at Dorothy. It soon became obvious that this look of reprimand was meant to elicit repentance. With humble apologies and an admission of recklessness and thoughtlessness, Dorothy was eventually allowed to go. Throughout the proceedings she had earnt the admiration of a young man, William Temple, who thought that her story was drivel but admired her verve and her loyalty to her brother. He caught her eye and his look must have said it all, because she gave him a rueful smile, before walking steadily out of the room.

Of course, it was now impossible for them to leave the country and so it was an anxious party that returned to Chicksands Priory. Dorothy settled back into their home, knowing that she had an admirer in William Temple, who had pledged himself to her as 'her affectionate servant', which was a way of asking to court her. However, William's father was a leading Cromwell supporter and had been a member of the Long Parliament. It was bound to be a courtship that neither family would approve of.

The distance of forty miles between London and Chicksands was not insurmountable. Servants devoted to both Dorothy and

William helped them to arrange meetings. At these meetings the couple told each other their stories with increasing confidence. Dorothy had been introduced to boorish men who took for granted that she would be flattered by their attentions. She found them dull and boring, and she had never been reassured by promises from aunts who said that once she was married to a suitor she would grow to love them. Life with William would not be leaden and grey but full of colour. She resolved to cope with the anxieties and the excitement of a courtship carried out in secret, but secretly dreaded the return of her father when the war ended.

At the end of the war, Sir Peter Osborne returned to Chicksands. His wife had died recently and much of the land surrounding the priory had been seized by Parliament. It was only because Sir Peter's brother-in-law had signed the death warrant for Charles I that he was not made destitute. Now poverty-stricken, he expected his daughter to make a good match. Sir Peter Osborne had imposed martial law when he was governor of Guernsey and so he did not mind dislike or even hatred. To some, he was a hard man. To Dorothy he was critical and expected obedience as he tried to find a husband who would maintain the family's position in society. Consequently, Dorothy was besieged by suitors but none had a chance of replacing William.

As the pressure to marry became more intense, William and Dorothy used their formidable charm and intelligence to continue seeing each other. They created a network of tradesmen to receive their letters and exhorted friends to collect the letters and deliver them. Dorothy sent vivid descriptions of the suitors that besieged her. She told William of the man who bemoaned her small dowry, until she waspishly commented that if she had one thousand pounds less then it would still be too much for him. She told him of Henry Cromwell, son of Oliver Cromwell, who had also visited her and whom she thought an insolent fool, debauched and ungodly.

In other letters Dorothy described the ingredients for her perfect match: 'Our humours must agree, he must not be so much a country gentleman as to understand nothing but hawks and dogs, and be fonder of either than of his wife; he must not be a town gallant neither, that lives in a tavern and cannot imagine how an hour should be spent without company unless it be in sleeping, that makes court to all the women he sees, thinks they believe him, and laughs and is laughed at equally. Nor a travelled Monsieur whose head is all feather inside and outside, that can talk of nothing but dances and duels, and has courage enough to wear slashes when everybody else dies with cold to see him. He must not be a fool of no sort, not peevish, nor ill-natured, nor proud, nor covetous; and to all this must be added, that he must love me and I him as much as we are capable of loving.'

Hope came slowly and with a sting in its tail. Sir Peter died in 1653 and then months later William Temple's father died. Henry Osborne was now head of the family. It was now that Dorothy's courage at the Isle of Wight, when she had saved Henry's life, brought its own reward. Henry was tempted to go along with what his father had instructed about the match, but he found it difficult to insist. He was grateful to her and did not see her as overemotional, unable to make her own decisions. Nevertheless, when he told her that he now agreed with the match, his voice was strained. He felt that he should restore the land around Chicksands Priory that had been lost, but with his one unmarried sister now betrothed, that ambition looked unachievable.

Preparations began for the couple's wedding. Dorothy travelled to London with Lady Peyton, a close friend of hers, to buy her trousseau. They stayed at a house in Drury Lane which, in the seventeenth century, was a place for intrigues but respectable. However, disease affected persons of all classes and when they discovered that another lodger had smallpox they swiftly fled. It was too late for Dorothy though – she had already contracted the disease. In the early days of the illness it was never clear how far it would develop and whether the sufferer would live or die. William despaired as all of his hopes and plans for the future seemed to unravel before him. Dorothy's friendship had been a thread that had run through his life for seven years and now he feared that it would disappear. Dorothy was strong, though, and little by little she recovered. When she was well enough, William didn't hesitate for an instant, despite the scarring left by smallpox, he married her.

In the years to come, little would be heard about Dorothy until she burst into the public spotlight as the Dutch and English vied for supremacy over the Channel. Charles II, who always had to appear kingly on a meagre budget, found paying for a navy problematic. Some of his poorly paid sailors succumbed to temptation and helped the Dutch in a raid on English shores that reached as far as the Medway. It was the worst defeat in the history of the Royal Navy and a humiliation for the king.

In the years to come, most English commentators despaired of ever beating the Dutch. Charles, however, was intent on provoking a war once the Royal Navy was battle-ready as a way to expunge the humiliation of the raid on the Medway. By this time, William was moving in powerful circles as a diplomat who had served the Crown abroad. Dorothy, fiery and charismatic as always, helped her husband where she was able and keenly applied herself to each diplomatic mission and matter of State. She agreed to cross the Dutch lines in the royal yacht, hoping to incite action that would break the treaty and lead to war. Whether she stood at the prow of the ship or not we will never know; however, Charles could not have found a better figurehead. The image of her, bravely standing like a Greek goddess of war, so roused public opinion in her support that a reluctant Parliament was dragged into a two-year war against the Dutch.

Most of her married life, however, was spent giving quiet support to her husband. William had a successful diplomatic career and Dorothy was a wise and clever counsellor to him.

Through highs and lows they were companions for one another. The marks left by smallpox must have stayed with her all her life, yet the only image we have of her, from the Dutch painter Gaspar Netscher, shows a placid middle-aged woman in flowing silk gowns with barely a mark on her skin. The couple faced a great deal of adversity together. Dorothy gave birth to seven children, five died in infancy and her daughter, Diana, died of smallpox at the age of fourteen. Only one child lived to adulthood. Their life together shows that they did indeed love each other as much as they were capable of loving.

23

THE COURTSHIP OF EDITH

When they heard the news of Harold's defeat at Hastings, Edith's family still held out hope. The northern earls might yet join together and chase the Normans out. But soon rumours reached them of a Norman army marching up the Icknield Way, seizing meat and corn from villages. The Normans expected dumb subservience and reacted brutally if villagers resisted them. By the time the army reached Bedford, it was clear that the Saxon people would not weather this storm in the same way that they had weathered Danish attacks. There was little resistance as the Normans took the town and what there was petered out quickly. Soon news came that London had surrendered as well.

In the months that followed, Edith's family heard of the massacres in the North of England, castles being built in London, Cambridge and Huntingdon. Work began on a castle in Bedford and the people came to know the heavy hand of the sheriff as men were forced to work clearing streets. The work on the castle gave the Normans a broad view of the river and took away the element of surprise in an attack. There were roads leading up to the river on either side and the Norman castle was built to dominate both sides.

The river was wilder and more untamed then. This was back when Edith was a spindly gawky nine year old and William the Conqueror had just invaded. The news came into the town in waves and Edith let it all wash over her. In her free time, she followed the river up to Kempston, where she played on half-submerged stones, jumping from one to another as she imagined that she was growing huge limbs. Each jump was no longer than a step from one small stone to another, but in her imagination each one was taking her from Bedford to London, to the North and, with one last leap, up into the sky. Or she would use her skill in swimming to recover small objects dropped from the side of boats. Sometimes her parents rewarded these efforts with just an affectionate ruffle of her unruly mop of hair, other times she was rewarded with a coin.

As her body started to blossom into adolescence, Edith realised that it was not just the river that cut Bedford into two but also the presence of the Normans. Slowly she came to understand the affect this was having on the town. First drop by drop, when she noticed that her father would not let her ask questions about neighbours who were copying the Normans by using French phrases. Then as a trickle, when she heard her parents arguing and her mother urging her father not to upset their masters. Then in a flood, as she started to look around herself, seeing in a new light how the crops were given to the Normans, the politeness that was shown to them, how everyone was trying to negotiate the tricky waters of their domination. For some this took the form of smouldering resentment – as with her family. Others relented and started to copy the manners and mores of the Normans.

It was the river that brought her Ralf. She had been swimming to catch beads from the river floor and when she surfaced, she was staring into bright watery blue eyes that gazed back at her with frank admiration. As a Norman, she spurned him – her family would be revolted. But he was relentless, he spent hours watching her by the water and she could feel his eyes burning into her back as she walked away from him. When she relented and shared a hunk of bread, she was surprised by the long silence between them, and she smiled tentatively at him. He was knowledgeable about the countryside and showed her birds and an empty tree trunk inhabited by bees. Not far from there was the apple tree where they began to meet regularly.

He was so unlike other men. Of course he recounted his successes at great speed, but he could also listen. And after listening there would be a brief pause before he nodded to show that he had understood what she had said. That deep look of contemplation. He gave her small tokens of his love – a bead, a dried flower, a lock of his hair that she kept in a box hidden in the wood. He wooed her and won her.

It was in the first days of spring that she noticed the changes in her body. She continued to meet Ralf underneath the apple tree. His first reaction was always to kiss her, stroking her face and whispering a pet name. He was always so happy to see her that she did not want to spoil it. She did not want to see his face fearful of the consequences. She knew that he would be happy about the baby but his family would have plans for him to marry another. Plans he would now have to destroy. It would not be easy for her family to find themselves tied to a Norman family as well, but of his love for her she had no doubt. She would take the distress of her family as a necessary evil and would marry him.

Then her mother started to whisper to her about the changes in her body. She knew she was pregnant and assumed that the father was a boy who had been Edith's friend since childhood. Her mother held her hand gently and told her that their larking about must result in marriage and that she would need to say something herself to the boy.

Shortly afterwards, Edith stood in a corner of the market, biting her lip tentatively when she saw Ralf. Harried by events, she ran up close to him, gazed up at him pleadingly and said quietly, 'I'm with child. Meet me at the apple tree tonight.' He looked shocked and then she saw him recover, his facial muscles relaxing as if he had pulled a mask across his face. There was no way of reading him. He left her alone for a couple of minutes and then strolled past the horse dealer's stall, pausing long enough to whisper, 'I will be there at dusk my sweet.'

It was with a certain amount of excitement that Edith waited for Ralf by their favourite tree. She knew they would face their families together and overcome disappointment on both sides. Maybe it would have been better to marry later but surely it was best to be honest. She was still light on her feet and climbed up the apple tree, clambering as high as she dared in order to break off a branch. She planned to tease him and give him the shock of his life by reaching down and poking him in the back with the branch or lowering the branch next to his face and stroking his strong Norman chin with the flowers. But it did not happen that way and later she wondered what would have become of her if she had carried out her plan and come down to earth to kiss him.

When Ralf arrived at the tree, she felt like she wanted this moment to take up more and more space in her heart, like a bubble of air growing underwater. She smiled fondly to herself as he looked around for her and felt inside his cloak. She was agile enough to move quietly round so that she could glance inside the cloak. What she had least expected to see was a knife, small and unburdened by any embellishment. Searching the familiar lines of his face, she saw that it was grim, unemotional and hardened.

Not moving a muscle, she stayed in the tree. The pain from the cramp was intense, a tickle on her nose became a torment and she dreaded that a growl from her stomach or a falling leaf would give her away. After an hour, he left, but she knew that this was just a reprieve and that he would silence her one way or another. She had been weak, a vessel to fill up to the brim with stupid ideas. All of that gallantry, the gentleness, the interest in her family, her feelings, her thoughts and emotions, had been a sham. All that time he had just been enjoying the thrill of the chase. She knew he intended to marry his Norman bride, and with her dead he would happily continue as before. Edith had never felt betrayal before. She was surprised that she did not feel upset or even ashamed. He must be made to pay for this. She did not know how she would do it, but from that moment she felt an implacable sense of vengeance.

She did know that she had to act quickly. She needed a space which was dominated by Anglo-Saxons and where there were few Normans keeping watch. A space in which she would be able to create enough anger against Ralf to bring about a reaction but without the Norman guards realising what was happening. She chose the market that was being held the next day.

There is a moment in diving underwater when you are poised between two worlds, the human world above and the water world underneath. Edith loved the feeling of power and freedom that she felt in such moments. She grasped hold of that feeling now as she stumbled up to one of the young men from the town who felt a constant sense of the indignity and shame about living under the Norman yoke. She grasped him just below the elbow, nodded in Ralf's direction and told him what had happened to her in a way that he wanted to hear. The news spread like wildfire through the market. She could tell who had been told the news by the look of horror on their face and then the hardening of their features.

Ralf was standing by a stall selling cheese. At first he was unconcerned by a couple of extra people standing next to him asking questions of the stall keeper, but as more people came and stood close to him, he suddenly became afraid. He tried to move in between two tall and bulky Anglo-Saxon men but they would not let him pass. Although he was cornered, to those just some yards away it would look like friendly fraternising with the locals. Edith could see that bodies were being used as cover to hide the jostling. Later she realised that a friendly hug had in fact been the moment when someone pulled out a knife from a cloak, then with a series of short, abrupt stabs, and one long flourish, Ralf was killed and he collapsed into a heap on the floor. Chaos ensued as Saxons began to throw over tables, shouting and jeering at the Norman guards. Edith's brother and father picked up Ralf's body, his cloak trailing along the ground as they dragged him into the privy of the local tavern. As they ran back out of the tavern, looks were exchanged with other Saxons. Gradually men became peaceable and willing to break up fights. They even started to restore order, picking up benches and tables from the centre of the market.

In the dead of night, the Saxons needed to act quickly. Of course, Ralf's body could not be left in the tavern to rot. In fact, it could not be found anywhere near Bedford as the consequences for the parish would be disastrous. Norman law punished the local community whether a murderer was found or not. So, using the moonlight to find a clear path, Edith's brother, father and her would-be sweetheart, the boy who had looked at her from afar, moved the body through the woods. They carried the body along paths hindered by branches and tendrils until they came to the boundary between Ravensden and Bedford parish. There his body was unceremoniously dumped, leaving the problem with the poor inhabitants of Ravensden who also hid the body and moved it overnight. The body was moved from place to place as quickly as possible.

Rumours were heard of what become of Ralf's body. He was moved around the parishes north of Bedford until it was realised that he was not much missed. Edith married her would-be sweetheart. The murder of Ralf was never mentioned between her and her husband or her and her family. Of Ralf, he was from a lower-rank Norman family and although Norman law favoured the Normans, his ability to run-up debts and ruin the maidservants of high-ranking Norman women was an irritant. It was a reflection of his life that no one could bring themselves to avenge his death.

24

GOSSIP

Once there was a man who lived in an obscure corner of Bedfordshire. He had gone to Eton and Cambridge. He looked set for a meteoric career but, although he kept in touch with current events, it never quite happened. The brilliant papers were never finished and the soirées were never well attended. Eventually he settled down to a quiet career in the Church in the countryside. He read avidly, collected books and found other ways of bringing excitement into his life.

Despite being a churchman, one of those ways was through his flamboyant fashion sense. Even by the standards of the day, which allowed men to dress as dandies, his style was eye-catching. On a dark October evening he attended a card game at a neighbour's house, peeling off his overcoat like the top layer of an onion to expose his grand clothes beneath, he flipped back his tailcoats, took a seat and accepted a glass of wine from a servant. Sipping the wine he commented, 'Mrs Hopkins looks miserable and who could be surprised. The gossip is that Mr Hopkins offered the maid five pounds to lie with him and when she refused he offered her ten pounds not to tell anyone.' All of the men laughed good-naturedly and one of his neighbours remarked that Mrs Hopkins was a good-sized woman who was stony-faced; indeed so stony-faced she had brought this trouble on herself. She was bovine, only interested in where the next meal came from. Laughing at their own wit, a good evening was had by all and the men, who played for only small amounts of money, and did nobody any harm, returned to their homes.

Two days later, a small boy returned to his cottage. His mother was known as the wise woman of the village. She always had the right thing to say to someone, whatever their troubles. The boy was sent out to play again straight away but not before he had caught a glimpse of Mrs Hopkins at their table. He had heard words said about her at school but she didn't look anything like that. As he returned home after playing, the two women were saying farewells on the doorstep. Then one woman whispered to the other, and they laughed companionably. A few days later, the dandy churchman received a letter through the post. In it was a coin and a note saying, 'a penny for keeping your thoughts to yourself, will bring you a fortune in heaven', laughing he pushed the strange letter into a bureau and promptly forgot about it.

Weeks later our clerical follower of fashion was playing billiards with his friends. His rag-coat disposed of in a corner, he revealed a silk waistcoat. Puffing his cigar, he blew out the smoke, and his chest swelled before he eyed the bets set on the side of the billiard table. He set up the shot and then, with all eyes on him, he leaned on his billiard cue and told the company, 'The maid of Mrs Hopkins has left to go to the manor but not before she gave Mr Hopkins a jolly good slap in the face.'

Quickly there was the response from his opponent: 'Did you see how black his face was and how Mrs Hopkins dodged in and out of the shops to avoid conversation?' He continued amongst raucous laughter, 'Indeed, Mr Hopkins came to dinner here and said not a word.'

The talk continued. Mrs Hopkins was pronounced sour-faced; Mr Hopkins, red-blooded and brazen; and the maid, a comely lass inviting lascivious thoughts. Impressed by their cleverness, generous feeling to all mankind and wide vocabulary, the men summoned a servant to bring their hats and coats and staggered home.

The wise woman told the maid that her door would always be open for her. And indeed it was needed. The young woman now had to cope with finding work again. Trying to find employment without what female servants referred to as 'maid-botherers' was notoriously difficult. Such men felt that they had a right to approach a maid and offer her money to lie with them. It was difficult to refuse them and keep a decent reference. When the silver-clad cleric received another envelope with a coin and the note, 'A penny for keeping your thoughts to yourself, will bring you a fortune in heaven', he raised an eyebrow this time, before flinging the note in the bureau drawer.

Several months later, our flamboyantly dressed man was at the head of the table for his own dinner party. Kitted out in the quite breath-taking outfit of waistcoats, silken scarves, a great coat and a hussar's hat, he was enjoying himself enormously. There was a flood of gossip and vintage wine. In amongst the flotsam and jetsam there was the story of Mr Hopkins' new maid, who said that her master had tried to put his hand under her petticoats. Resorting to drift-wood gossip from other villages, he told his guests of a Mrs Smith who lay with her husband for three weeks and thought she must be pregnant even though he had never touched her. The cleric's good friend was sitting next to him. By now red-faced, he snorted and affectionately told the snappy dresser that he was a connoisseur of title-tattle. They laughed and discussed heartily the Widow Woods who everyone knew was a kept mistress.

Over the years the man received more of the cryptic notes with small coins, and he became more jaded with each one. The women of the village prepared his food, his clothes, cleaned his house and laundered his clothes. For him, they were like silent spectres who oiled the wheels of his everyday life, making sure he did not have to do anything commonplace, let alone monotonous, greasy or grimy. He thought of them very little, unless it was something to do with what he wanted or needed. Each word of gossip he uttered was like a feather thrown into the wind, impossible to recapture it and undo the consequences, but this was of no relevance to him. Of course, he would not demean his talk with other men with the word 'gossip'.

And so the cleric knew the coins were trying to say something but knew not what. He ignored them; leaving the coins to slowly gather dust. As he grew older and infirm, he no longer had the strength or the inclination to pry into others' lives. Gossip had once been his currency – offered as part of a night's entertainment – and without it his friends slowly abandoned him. He had one reluctant visitor – a slightly ashamed nephew who had been bullied by aunts to stay in touch. His future would be much improved by a bequest in the man's will.

Mostly alone now, the women in his household listened to an endless stream of prattle: 'I've been having lots of trouble with my legs. Well I told my young nephew, you know, that his plan of building bridges and whatnot in the army would come to nothing. An engineer!' He paused briefly as his maid brought in his coffee.

'But the young people today. I need a new kind of cream for my face, I tried that one and it made me sneeze. I have a very delicate constitution you know. I can't tell you the suffering that I've had.' The maid frowned slightly as she concentrated on pouring out his milk; he was not forgiving of even the slightest spill.

'The best physicians have all seen me and none of them can help. I have half a mind to talk to the bishop to tell him about it.

What? Not the face cream, you stupid woman. I can't sleep, you know. I have to publish my book and my journal before I've gone. I need a new waistcoat, what colour should I ask for?' Like pouring rain on a cold February morning, the cleric's talk carried on relentlessly.

His eventual decline and death was swift and painless, and his servants felt the relief of not having to listen to his talk and a sadness that the end of a life was worth so little. As a respectable member of the clergy, a funeral was planned but few expected it to be well attended. His circle had all forsaken him as his health grew worse and those of a lower rank had little respect from him. Only the nephew, who hoped for a mention in the cleric's will, had made it to the church on the day set for the funeral.

The nephew entered the church nervously. He was a diffident young man who wanted to buy a commission for the army and was uncomfortable with the predicament he felt himself to be in. Fortunately for him the bishop asked few questions and was eager to perform the ceremony as if a saint had lived among them. Such aplomb had served him well over the years and he ignored the fact that only the man's nephew attended the funeral in full – a few villagers poking their heads into the church out of curiosity before going back to their work.

The bishop had a busy diary and so rattled through the order of service at a fair pace. However, he knew when to show due respect and had, what he reckoned, was a very impressive sermon ready for his assemblage. He was not going to be shaken by the fact that he had just one person in the audience. Truly a man who would have been a successful actor if he had not decided to grasp the bishop's crook instead, he reasoned that an audience of one was still an audience. He started his speech in a low and steady voice, intoning the difficulties of life as a priest in rural Bedfordshire. He was getting more confident now, his body language was more relaxed and he felt that the nephew was ready for a bit of showmanship. 'I found within his bureau proof of how much he was loved by parishioners. All of them were poor, but their love for him was so great that they gave him pennies over the years to show their gratitude.' With a flourish, he took a purse and poured the pennies given by the victims of the man's gossip out onto the lectern. The bishop looked up earnestly with an air of expectation, saying, 'He was the soul of discretion amongst his flock as the Lord will testify.' Immediately a jagged flash of lightning swept across the sky. The cleric's nephew briefly saw a trace of the lightning in the church window before the bishop threw himself from the pulpit on to the church floor in fear.

Fearing that the Lord had indeed testified to such an outrageous untruth they both settled down to pray in earnest and so were unaware of the danger approaching them. It was the wise woman who was first aware of the risk to the village. She was hanging out her washing and caught the slightly acrid smell of smoke in the air. When she looked up she thought she could see a hint of black smoke rising up above the rooftops. Throwing the clothes pegs to the ground, she hitched up her skirts and ran down the street, hammering on doors with her fists and calling for help. The word 'fire' leapt from mouth to mouth as the villagers hastily looked for the source of the fire before it could destroy their homes. When eventually the hapless bishop discovered that the church was on fire, he ran out to find villagers already in the process of dowsing it. Amongst those offering help were Mrs Smith and Mrs Hopkins – despite their frailty – and many others whom the wise woman had counselled over the years.

The villagers created a chain of people stretching from the village pond to the church, quickly handing along pails and saucepans full of water. Luckily the lightning had struck the body of the church rather than the steeple and, although the fire had started to spread, the use of fire-hooks and hand-held water squirts had put out much of it. When the flames were dowsed and the risk was averted, the villagers looked at each other with relief and the wise woman was pleased to see that many of the women who had stayed out of the public eye because of gossip, were now earnestly chatting to one another.

The wise woman grew frailer as she became older. Her son remembered a stream of woman who came to her for advice and companionship, and from the nods and smiles he and his family received, he knew what it was like to grow up well-respected. There is no headstone, no monument to the woman. All that remained was the wisdom that she passed down through her family, that a life made up of small acts of kindness and learning from other people is not a life wasted.

Ironically for the cleric, his greatest piece of gossip was the story of his own funeral. It was remembered as the day when the Lord let it be known how he felt about gossip. Villagers would enjoy telling the story, explaining how the cleric lived for gossip and how the bishop stood at the lectern telling untruths about the man's goodness. They ended their story by pointing at the rebuilt church and saying, 'Well, the bishop said the Lord would give a sign and he sure got one.'

25

THE ROLL OF HONOUR

Eileen Garrett was a peculiar child. Silent to her teachers and to her aunt, she seemed to bear no particular talents, yet she would become internationally famous. She had no attachment to Bedfordshire, yet by the end of her life, she would become inextricably linked with the county. Born in County Meath, Ireland, in 1893, her parents both committed suicide shortly after her birth and she went to live with an aunt. Grieving and guilt-ridden, her aunt found the child's blank face infuriating and she became increasingly angry. Soon the two were locked into a pattern of the aunt's anger and the child's withdrawal, with only short periods of peace. She lived in a repressive atmosphere in which the smallest gesture could result in recriminations and tears.

Her aunt was not physically cruel but her power over Eileen seemed to rest on whims and to be totally arbitrary. Eileen retreated into a bubble and created a fantasy world, with different personalities living in her head. Her dreams seemed to merge with real life, and different dreamscapes, lives and colours would float through her head unbidden, leaping into her imagination until she lost track of who or where she was. She had believed herself to be a medium as a child, and after her marriage, to Clive Barry, she found reason to return to that belief. She had three sons and a daughter. All three of the sons died young and Eileen needed something to give her a reason to live. She was drawn into the world of being a medium as a way of dulling the pain of bereavement. Soon she found that she could help the bereaved find comfort and it brought her unexpected fulfilment.

In contrast, Olivia grew up in Berwick, East Lothian. The daughter of well-established middle-class parents, she had a comfortable childhood. Her father was a doctor and the family moved to Fareham in Hampshire as his career developed. Her early life was full of ponies and close friends who she stayed in touch with throughout much of her adult life. As well as wide-open spaces to explore with friends, she found quiet woods that were carpeted with bluebells or leaves, depending on the season. She was expected to make a good match and so when dashing Carmichael Irwin courted her, she started to see that she could both please her parents and set out on a life of excitement. It was not exactly a whirlwind romance but, less than two years after meeting, the couple were married. They moved to Long Acre, which was in Putnoe Lane in Bedford.

By this time, her husband was working on airships. As was the habit amongst men of his class at the time, he was called Irwin in a gruff manner by his colleagues as a way of showing acceptance and affection. Over the next few years, Irwin helped to develop the new technology of air flight, a technology which had been crucial for the Allies in securing victory in the Great War. Now the Allies wanted to keep their advantage and continue to explore this machinery. They envisaged an airship network linking Britain with its colonies and dominions.

Later, Eileen would say that she received a vision of an airship ablaze over Holland Park, struggling to maintain flight. She would say that she wrote to Sefton Brancker, the Director of Civil Aviation, warning him not to continue with the development of the R100 and R101. We will never know what Sir Sefton's response really was, but the story that he scoffed and threw the letter away took on an air of truth.

Irwin was not transferred to the R101 project straightaway. He had been given the important task within the Royal Airship Works of command of the R33. After four years in mothballs, the R33 ship flew to Pulham in Norfolk for aerodynamic testing but it broke free from its mast and was blown towards the Netherlands. However, Irwin was still seen as a safe pair of hands, and was moved to the R101 as captain in 1929.

Irwin did not take the role of captain lightly, and Olivia listened patiently to him as he described all of the technical details over the course of the following year. The couple did not have any children and Olivia had always known that she provided a house and home for him. Olivia saw her work as supporting him and listened patiently to his plans without asking many questions. She did not understand the technical details but she was very shrewd. Unconvinced by his outward self-confidence and bonhomie, she spoke to him directly and noticed how, when lost in his own thoughts, there was a pursing of the lips and a shrug of the shoulders that had not been there before.

Irwin said nothing publicly about any doubts but, before the flight, Olivia was not alone in a feeling of foreboding. Chief Coxswain George Hunt told his family that he feared that he would never return. One engineer was said to be so afraid of the flight that he drove off on his motorcycle and distractedly drove into the path of a lorry. As Rigger Walter Radcliffe left his home, his son cried out, 'I do not have a daddy'. Even Sir Sefton may have had his doubts in a quiet, dark moment, as friends said that he had a horoscope, which showed a blank after 1930.

The R101 departed from Cardington on the evening of 4 October 1930. Its intended destination was Karachi, then part of British India, with a refuelling stop in Ismailia in Egypt. Irwin gave the order for the R101 to cast off from the mast at 18:36 to a cheer from the crowd that had gathered to witness the event. George Hunt, the coxswain who feared this journey would be his last, gently backed from the tower and, as another ton of ballast was shed, the engines were opened up to about half power. As the ship began to climb away, the rigger, Walter Radcliffe, was busy with a series of checks on the airship. With the light from the sun already dimming, the shadow it cast over the landscape seemed to swallow the fields of parsley and white clover. The huge construction moved ponderously over the landscape, its drone announcing its imminent arrival. At its approach everyone stopped and craned their necks skyward. It was a symbol of the might of the Empire, majestic and awe-inspiring.

At one o'clock in the early hours of the next morning, Irwin sent a message describing their course and speed, altimeter height and air temperature. He also described how, 'After an excellent supper our distinguished passengers smoked a final cigar and, having sighted the French coast, have now gone to bed to rest after the excitement of their leave takings.'

At seven minutes past two, the airship was passing Beauvais. A small boy who had pestered his parents to let him stay awake was found slumped over the windowsill and, as his father picked him up, he saw the ship begin a long dive, seemingly heading towards the ground. Irwin was roused from a short catnap by the dive and rushed towards the control room, grasping hold of the iron framework. George Hunt, who had been in the control room, was dusting himself down and Walter Radcliffe – injured by falling furniture – was nursing a deep cut to his arm when the airship steadied itself, although now at a much lower altitude.

But within moments there was a collective gasp as the rooms tilted again. Furniture began to slide and crewmembers stumbled and fell. There was a sudden shudder to one side. George Hunt in the control room reacted immediately by pulling the elevator up. The captain rang the order for all engines to reduce speed. The bells were heard and George Hunt moved forward from the control room to the crew's quarters. He passed crewmember Disley and warned, 'We're down lads'. This comment was to become one of the most famous comments during the whole disaster, signalling the attempt to make an emergency landing.

Marguerite Tassi, in Allone, was woken by the roar of the engines and an explosion. A second and larger explosion followed and shattered all of the windows in the house, lighting the sky with flame. She dressed hastily and ran in the direction of the fire.

In the second and fatal dive, there was no way that the crew could have reacted quickly enough to avoid a collision with the ground. Later inspections would find that the sudden move to one side had torn a rent in the material in the upper part of the nose and the gas bags were damaged. The airship hit the ground just outside a wood on the edge of Allone, two miles south-west of Beauvais. As it hit the ground, the starboard engine car was twisted round, meeting the gas from the damaged gas bags. The outer cover quickly caught light and peeled away, fed by the five-and-a-half million cubic feet of explosive hydrogen carried by the airship.

Marguerite ran towards the airship until she reached an intense wall of heat. With the firestorm inside, only a few people near the exits in certain parts of the ship were lucky enough to be able to escape. A man also stood watching and Marguerite halted mutely next to him. The fury of the flames held them both in thrall. She did not speak, unable to know how to start. He wore a tattered uniform. He was tall and she could see that he had hurt his arm from the way that he held it. Suddenly they both saw a figure in the fire, and when she turned to the man, he was running towards the flames. She never saw him again. At exactly the same time, a member of staff who was working late in Irwin's office back in Bedfordshire noticed that his phone flashed, as though someone was ringing him. When he picked up the phone line was dead.

The fire continued to burn into the next day. The battle to be the first in the race for the airways was over. When the flames were extinguished, it was an even more forlorn sight. The giant airship was now a beached Leviathan with its stainless-steel girders twisted and anguished. The skeletal, blackened remains subsumed the landscape, with its reminder of the tragedy that had occurred. For a while it was no longer a quiet country town, but a resting place for the dead. The remains of the airship were to remain where it had fallen until well into 1931, becoming a haunt for air accident investigators and day trippers who wanted to see the near-perfect skeleton of the largest airship in the world.

Two days after the crash, Eileen Garrett was holding a séance in the National Laboratory of Psychical Research, set up four years earlier by Harry Price, a well-known psychic investigator. Price, his secretary, and journalist Ian D. Coster had arranged a sitting with Eileen, hoping to establish a spirit contact with the recently deceased writer Sir Arthur Conan Doyle.

Shortly after the sitters had gathered in the séance room, Eilleen went into a trance. Instead of making contact with the novelist, however, the sitters heard a voice announcing himself as Flight Lieutenant Irwin. In a voice at first flat and practical, and then increasingly dramatic, she said, 'I must do something about it ... Engines too heavy. Scuttling to safety. And this idea of new elevators ... problems with oil pipe ... Flying to low altitude. Load too great for long flight ... Cruising speed bad and ship badly swinging. Severe tension on the fabric, which is chafing ... Engines wrong. Never reached cruising altitude – same in trials. Too short trials. We never had enough time to know the ship properly. Weather bad but still told we had to go.

Fabric holding too much water. Cannot trim. On no, we are far too low, almost scraping rooftops'.

The reporter who took this amazing communication in short-hand at first resented the intrusion of Irwin, captain of the R101, when he had expected the voice of Sir Arthur Conan Doyle. But he was soon to realise that he had a much bigger story and it was now that Eileen achieved international fame, or maybe it was infamy, as the bodies of the dead had not yet reached the shores of Great Britain to receive a state funeral.

A few more days passed as travel arrangements were discussed by the British and French governments. The bodies, placed in coffins draped with the Union Jack, were then taken by train to Boulogne. From there the coffins were carried by HMS *Tempest* to Dover, where a special train took them to Victoria Station. In a full state funeral honouring the dead, the public showed their sympathy in a typically British way. They honoured them by queuing, waiting patiently for hours to file past the coffins lying in state at Westminster Hall. The queue snaked along the Embankment, reaching as far as Vauxhall Bridge.

Then the coffins were moved to Bedford. Behind two RAF vehicles walked the relatives of the dead. Irwin's wife was amongst them. After a harrowing wait and time for the news to sink in, they now walked subdued but resolute. Olivia could not help thinking that she had known that the last flight was doomed – she had the gift of knowing – but had been so helpless to stop it. Also in the procession, George Hunt's widow had shared the feeling of foreboding and Walter Radcliffe's widow remembered her son's words as her husband left their home for the last time – 'I don't have a daddy.'

In line, behind the relatives, were Air Ministry and Air Council officials, then the third watch of R101 and finally a long line of cars drew up at the end of the procession. They walked the two miles to Cardington Village, where a space had been prepared in the church-yard. All forty-eight dead were finally laid to rest in a special grave.

But for many this was not the end of the story. There was a feeling of incredulity, verging on denial, amongst the public. How could what was, without doubt, the greatest nation in the world, have failed to launch the R101 airship? Was there foul play, incompetence or something supernatural to explain our failure? Bedford, and Cardington in particular, continued to grieve quietly. A memorial to the dead was erected in the cemetery of St Mary's church in Cardington. Shaped much like a coffin itself, it was built in the Classical style with simple columns and the symbol of the RAF dominating one face. An inscription reads, 'Herein lies the bodies of forty-eight officers and men who perished in HM Airship R101 at Beauvais France' before a roll call of the dead. It was impossible to give each man an individual burial place, as the fire had been so fierce that their remains were indistinguishable. The memorial hopes to give a roll of honour to the men who lost their lives in the flames.

For some of those who had lost dear friends and family, they clung to the stories of Eileen Garrett. Major Oliver Villiers lost many friends on the flight. These included Sefton Brancker, the Director of Civil Aviation; Major Scott, one of the designers of the mooring masts; and Captain Irwin. He participated in further séances with Garrett, claiming that he had long talks with lost friends. Dialogue seemingly revealed technical details that only those involved with the R101 project would know. Whether this was a real link to lost friends or a fragile thread that gave him the semblance of a connection with those who had died, we will never know.

The huge airship hangars are impossible to miss on the Bedfordshire landscape. For many years the hangars were allowed to deteriorate. A dilapidated blot on the landscape, patches of rust appeared on the sides of the buildings, and holes in the roofs meant that the buildings were condemned as unsafe. Not only did Bedfordshire carry the burden of knowing that so many had died working on the R101 but now the hangars were becoming an eyesore.

The dedication of villagers in Cardington has changed all of this. One of the hangars has been completely restored. It is a source of great pride and has given the impetus and motivation to restore the second. The initial charm of the hangars is the glamour of filming, using the cathedral-like heights within. But for those with roots within Bedfordshire, they are also a reminder of a time when air travel was not commonplace. A time when air travel was exotic and dangerous, and forty-eight brave men lost their lives in pursuit of it.

26

The Merry Monk

Brother Peter stood outside of the bakery hesitating. Shortly, he would be walking to Warden Abbey and he reasoned that maybe he needed a sweet treat to bolster him for the journey. Brother Peter was a Cistercian monk and spent most of his time overseeing the work of the order's tenant farmers. Warden Abbey was formed less than a century after the invasion of William the Conqueror. Since then the abbey had grown rich and, although the order was dedicated to a simple life of manual labour in the fields, most of the monks spent little time on the myriad of tasks needed to keep the fields fruitful.

Brother Peter was middle-aged, not quite as slim as he had used to be, and with not quite as much hair as he used to have. Despite the plethora of dietary rules that were part of the religious life, on a fast day he managed to eat more than a labourer who worked from dawn to dusk toiling the fields. On a normal day he relished visits to the order's tenants, testing their honey and their cheeses. He did not bother himself with thoughts of the turn of the seasons. The peasants would keep the hedge boundaries clear throughout the year. They would also plough, sow, reap and thresh.

One of the farmers had a daughter named Jane. Jane was stunning, with bright red hair that, when she was at home, flowed in waves down her shoulder, although she kept it discretely covered when out in public. She was sociable and, when she visited the village on market day, she knew how to make people laugh at just the right point in a sale to help her get the right price. Although ambitious, she was also well liked, as over the years, people from the village and surrounding farms had grown to trust her. She wanted to marry well and set up some trade on her own. Her neighbours reckoned that if a good marriage was what she wanted then good for her.

Brother Peter knew of Jane. He had caught glimpses of her. Those glimpses had been enough to place her, with her hourglass figure, in his mind as a shimmering dream of all that he had denied himself with promises of leading a celibate life. And he was making strenuous efforts not to see her. The more he saw of that voluptuous figure and sweet smile, the more he imagined her hair flowing on a pillow and the less reason he could see for remaining celibate. It was seriously interfering with his attempt to pray. Every time he closed his eyes he thought of her and sometimes he had to open his eyes again with haste to stop his mind wandering in sensual directions.

Adding extra tinder to the flames was the fact that harvests for the past two years had been low for her father and he owed the abbey money. Brother Peter had a self-confidence that was made of iron and impervious to reality. He felt sure that if he could make some compromises regarding celibacy then Jane would be more than happy to help his wishes become reality. And offering her some money would just make him even more attractive.

Basically, Brother Peter wanted nothing more or less than to take her virginity.

But when he offered Jane his terms, the ambitious girl had to think on her feet – she did not want him calling in debts to the abbey but neither did she have any intention of going along with his wishes. So she told him that she feared that she would go to hell for such an act. It seemed a long shot but she asked him to take pity on her and give her the money anyway.

'Tush,' said the monk. 'Thou needst not doubt. If thou wert in hell, I could sing thee out.' Jane concluded that he was not worried if she were to go to hell.

'Then,' said Jane, 'thou shalt have thy request.' She looked down demurely but inside she felt quite murderous.

Brother Peter, meanwhile, was as happy as a fox in a chicken coop, and by the lascivious look on his face, he was ready to complete the bargain there and then.

'But one thing,' Jane said, with a blank look on her face. 'I do desire first, that you will bring me an angel of money.'

With a touch that started by her ear and slid down but didn't quite reach her breast, Brother Peter breathed quietly in her ear, 'Tush, no money shall part my love and me.'

And so they arranged a meeting in a room in the tavern. However, our heroine asked the tavern-keeper's daughter to set up a ground floor as their bedroom. This room had a water well off the far wall that they used to draw water for cooking and cleaning, and she hung a heavy cloth in front of it.

It is difficult to look as if you welcome a man's touch when in fact it is as cold and clammy as wet porridge, but somehow Jane managed it. When Brother Peter strolled in with a skip and a swagger, he held his little bag of money. 'Good morrow, fair maid,' he declared, with an expansive gesture as if to show her what a wonderful body she would soon be able to enjoy. He gently, and with great aplomb, placed the bag of money on a shelf.

Jane had found a dress that attempted to make her look drab, but Brother Peter was not put off. He stroked her hair and kissed her face, and was just in the act of grabbing the dress in handfuls in the spirit of not wasting any time, when there was a polite little knock at the door. The tavern-keeper's daughter opened the door, peered timidly into the room and said in a small voice, 'Begging your pardon, there's some ale here for you both,' placing a flagon on a table. She returned just a minute later, scuttling over to the table and coughing while she explained that she had forgotten to take away any dirty beakers. Brother Peter, however, was unable to see the wink and the accompanying smirk aimed at Jane as she deftly moved through the doorway with the beakers, turning quickly to shut the door. Immediately the door was shut, Brother Peter rubbed his hands together gleefully, smiled at Jane, and seconds later she was pinned against the wall. His bright face was looming towards Jane's enthusiastically when there was another knock on the door. He stood poised to shoo the tavern-keeper's daughter out when she explained that Jane's father was in the tavern looking for her.

Brother Peter's eyes bulged almost out of his forehead and his hands flapped ineffectually by his sides. Why had she told her father where she would be? She was an obedient daughter; of course she had to answer her father's questions.

'Alas, where shall I run to hide me till he be gone?' the monk asked imploringly.

'Behind the cloth run thou,' Jane said, pointing. 'And there my father cannot thee see.'

She did not need to say any more, the monk leapt through the cloth and into the well behind it. There was a great splosh and then a weak voice cried, 'My sweetheart, I am in a well.'

'Well I know it,' the pun obviously intended. 'Thou sayst thou couldst sing me out of hell, now prithee sing thy self out of the well.'

So the monk sang plaintively. Seeing no effect come from his efforts, he called, 'Oh help me out, or I shall be drowned.'

'I see your ardour is cooled.'

He shouted back, 'I was never so fooled.' Now he became bold and belligerent: 'I never was served so before. For sweet Saint Francis' sake, on his disciple some pity take.'

At this, Jane could take no more; she opened the cloth and stared down at him. Challenging him, she said, 'Saint Francis never taught his scholars to tempt young maids.'

Brother Peter stared up at her, open-mouthed and unable to say anything, at which she took pity on him and went to find a rope to help him out. He pulled his robes into shape and, avoiding looking at her, he asked for his money back.

'Good sir,' she said and, becoming more than a little angry as she said it, she appeared to grow taller. 'If you do not leave, I'll make you pay for fouling the tavern's water.'

The monk went all along the street, dripping wet like a new-washed sheep. Both young and old praised the maid Jane for the witty prank that she had played. The episode did not hurt her chances of a good marriage and within a year she was married to a respectable merchant.

The village of Old Warden now shows little sign of the medieval prosperity and the chaos of the Dissolution of the Monasteries. The abbey was dissolved by Henry VIII and the estate was sold for £389 16s 6d. The new owner demolished most of the buildings in 1552 to sell the materials, and then built a new red-brick mansion. A fragment of that mansion stands today and is owned by the Landmark Trust, who rescued and renovated it.

The building is now stranded in quiet fields; the farmland is flat, airy and full of promise. The patterned brickwork and chimney would once have screamed wealth and power. The surroundings give it the air of a minor royal: proud and slightly forlorn. Inside it is luxurious, with open fireplaces and heavily moulded oak ceilings, but outside is like looking at only one shard of what used to be a kaleidoscope.

27

THE SILENT SENTINELS

Roxton has always been a leafy place, one which gives trees and green-ery a place. There was a time when the people shared the land with the trees, saying prayers whenever they cut the higher branches or chopped one down to use for furniture, ships or enclosures for animals. There was a reverence for the trees in those prayers. A reverence for their ability to take sunlight and turn it into something mankind could use. But as time went on they forgot to say such prayers. In fact they seemed to feel that they owned the trees and some humans went as far as thinking that they owned other people. For beings who live as long as trees, this only caused sadness. A human being's life is so short that it is a shame if it is short and harsh as well. For the trees living close to churches and places of worship, the changes were easier to bear. People put their feelings of envy and hurt to one side, and when they gazed at the trees with longing for a better world, the trees were sensitive to that yearning and able to sooth them.

And so the trees looked after the humans as they looked after their own saplings. They noticed changes in their moods and feel-ings. In the late spring one year it was particularly noticeable. As the humans left the church, everything was bathed in clear sunlight and there was a light breeze. The children hopped and skipped in the sunshine but the adults were dour and in a grey mood. They huddled together. Some puffed themselves up and talked earnestly to the others but most were bewildered, angry, downcast.

The trees then noticed that if a young man appeared at church wearing a peaked hat and trousers ironed so that there were no creases, the humans would cluster around him shaking his hand, keen to touch him and show pride in him. Then the trees would see no more of him. The pride was hollow. In the weeks and months to come the young men slowly disappeared one by one and the women would offer up prayers which rippling upwards and brushed past the leaves of the trees. The trees were as conscious of the sadness as they were of the sun, the rain and the moonlight.

The first human to come to the trees did so late at night. Clutching a piece of paper, she curled up at the bottom of a tree and sobbed. The tree saw the piece of paper but forgave the humans. It hoped that the paper had been made with the veneration and respect that they had shown the trees in the past. As the woman sobbed and sniffed, the tree felt for her and sent a couple of leaves to comfort her, trying in vain to curl its roots to cradle her. Every so often women would appear, sometimes clutching a small piece of paper rolled up in their hands, sometimes a larger one. These pieces of paper all had funny black marks on them and the women would stare at these marks in disbelief. Their feelings were like the colours of the autumn leaves, some were blazing in red-hot anger, some were green with envy for others who were untouched, some were a muddy brown, dulled by the worry of how to get by.

Dorothy had a fine brood of boys. When she visited the trees the first time, she cried and left weary but determined to be brave. The second time, she was wracked with sobs. But on the third time, her anger was so red-hot that she clenched her fists and pounded on the tree's bark until her knuckles bled. Together the trees sent murmurings through their leaves to heal her. Eventually the susurrus murmurings reached her and she stayed there till the early hours of the morning, rocking herself in time to them.

After many years the men began to return to Roxton. They all
looked as if their thoughts were somewhere else and some of
them were missing arms and legs, and used sticks to get around.
The trees were very sad for them – they knew it must be worse
than losing a branch. And so from that time, the trees offered
their trunks and their branches to support the roof of the church.
The trees sustained the congregation of the church by becoming
part of the building and the people of Roxton found clarity and
peace. Each tree sent their branches spiralling upwards to offer
their support and love to the community. A community that, like
many others, had given so much in the war to end all wars.

This story aims to capture the spirit of Roxton Congregational
church, which was built in the nineteenth century rather than
after the First World War. It is a beautiful building with a thatch
overhang supported by tree trunks. When I first entered the
churchyard, immediately enveloped by birdsong, I was struck by
how picturesque and quaint the building is with two slender trees
looming over and guarding it. I realised that its simplicity is deceptive and that the building is cleverly built to create this illusion.

As I got to know more of the details, the building became like a good companion with its rustic benches and Gothic details. There is more, however, as the building responds to all moods. In a joyful mood, I can stand by the slow curve of the hill and overlook parkland. In a more sombre mood, there is a small recess built into the outside of the church using sticks to create patterns and vaulting and cones as embellishments at the top of wooden columns. The effect is uplifting, like that of a tactful and comforting silence, and provides a wonderful sense of contentment.

BIBLIOGRAPHY

BOOKS

Child, Frances James, *The English and Scottish Popular Ballads* (Houghton, Mifflin and Company, 1886–98)

Farmer, David, *Oxford Dictionary of Saints* (Oxford University Press, 2011 edn)

Godber, Joyce, *History of Bedfordshire* (White Crescent Press, 1970)

Pevsner, Nikolaus, *The Buildings of England: Bedfordshire, Huntingdon and Peterborough* (Penguin, 1968)

Steinhardt, Mark, *Murder in Flitwick Wood* (White Hart Press, 2008)

Tongue, Ruth, *Forgotten Folk-tales of the English Counties* (Routledge & K. Paul, 1970)

Westwood, Jennifer and Simpson, Jacqueline, *The Lore of the Land* (Penguin, 2006)

WEBSITES

bbc.co.uk/history

Gutenberg.org

Urbanlegends.about.com

About the Author and Illustrator

JEN FOLEY is a professional storyteller and runs 'Time Weavers' historical workshops. She has a background in radio journalism and public relations, and now writes her own stories for performance (mainly featuring feisty heroines and cunning aplenty). She lives in Bedford.

TONY HUNT is an artist and illustrator, who works in a variety of media and enjoys the challenge of working from life. He has exhibited widely and lives in East Hertfordshire.

Society for Storytelling

Since 1993, the Society for Storytelling has championed the art of oral storytelling and the benefits it can provide – such as improving memory more than rote learning, promoting healing by stimulating the release of neuropeptides, or simply great entertainment! Storytellers, enthusiasts and academics support and are supported by this registered charity to ensure the art is nurtured and developed throughout the UK.

Many activities of the Society are available to all, such as locating storytellers on the Society website, taking part in our annual National Storytelling Week at the start of every February, purchasing our quarterly magazine *Storylines*, or attending our Annual Gathering – a chance to revel in engaging performances, inspiring workshops, and the company of like-minded people.

You can also become a member of the Society to support the work we do. In return, you receive free access to *Storylines*, discounted tickets to the Annual Gathering and other storytelling events, the opportunity to join our mentorship scheme for new storytellers, and more. Among our great deals for members is a 30% discount off titles in the *Folk Tales* series from The History Press website.

For more information, including how to join, please visit

www.sfs.org.uk

Lightning Source UK Ltd.
Milton Keynes UK
UKOW06f2147110915

258477UK00001B/4/P